Q

MW01588298

DDC®

Lotus® 1·2·3®
Release 4
for Windows™

Iris Blanc

Dictation Disc Company
14 East 38 Street, New York, NY 10016

INTRODUCTION

The DDC Quick Reference Guide for Lotus 1-2-3 Release 4 for Windows will save you hours searching through technical manuals for keystrokes and mouse actions.

Lotus 1-2-3 Release 4 for Windows tasks may be accessed in several ways:

- Using the mouse for the main menu

- Using the mouse for SmartIcons

- Using keystrokes for the main menu

- Using "Classic keystrokes" (the traditional method used in earlier Lotus 1-2-3 releases)

Tasks are listed in alphabetical order, and the template featured on the back cover provides a fast reference to Lotus 1-2-3 Release 4 for Windows "Classic keystrokes."

(continued...)

ii

TABLE OF CONTENTS

(continued...)

TABLE OF CONTENTS (continued)

(continued...)

iv

TABLE OF CONTENTS (continued)

(continued...)

TABLE OF CONTENTS (continued)

(continued...)

vi

TABLE OF CONTENTS (continued)

(continued...)

TABLE OF CONTENTS (continued)

(continued...)

viii

TABLE OF CONTENTS (continued)

(continued...)

TABLE OF CONTENTS (continued)

(continued...)

x

TABLE OF CONTENTS (continued)

(continued...)

TABLE OF CONTENTS (continued)

(continued...)

xii

TABLE OF CONTENTS (continued)

(continued...)

TABLE OF CONTENTS (continued)

(continued...)

xiv

TABLE OF CONTENTS (continued):

(continued...)

Before You Begin...

You should become familiar with **Introductory Basics,** which includes illustrations and descriptions of Lotus for Windows screens, as well as definitions for terms used throughout this guide.

In addition, you should become familiar with basic cursor movements using the keyboard and the mouse (pages xix, xx), "SmartIcons" and their corresponding commands (page 132) and the highlighting/selecting procedures *(See INTRODUCTORY BASICS, page xvi).*

It is my hope this guide will help you use Lotus 1-2-3 Release 4 for Windows with ease.

IRIS BLANC

Author:	Iris Blanc
Technical Editing and Consulting:	Glenn S. Davis
English Editor:	Rebecca J. Fiala
Editor:	Kathy Berkemeyer
Graphic Design and Layout:	Chassman/Han Graphics

(continued...)

xvi

INTRODUCTORY BASICS
The Lotus 1-2-3 Release 4 Windows Screen

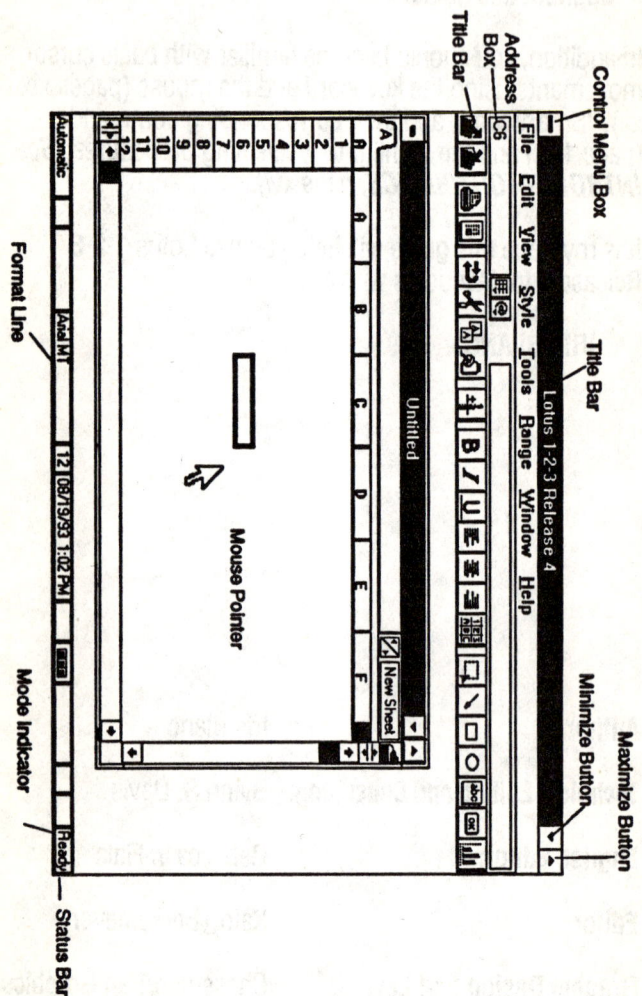

(continued...)

Windows Screen Parts Descriptions

- **Control Menu Box** Clicking once opens menu; clicking twice exits Lotus 1-2-3 Release 4 for Windows.

- **Title Bar** Displays program title and named worksheet. Pressing right mouse button while pointing to a SmartIcon shows its description.

- **Maximize Button** Clicking once expands window to a full screen. (After window is maximized, the Maximize button is replaced with Restore button .)

- **Main Menu Bar** Displays main selections from which pull-down menus may be accessed.

- **Format Line** Displays formatting information about a selected cell or range of cells.

- **Mode Indicator** Displays "mode" or status of the program.

- **Address Box** Displays location of the current cell.

- **Edit Line** Displays characters or formulas as you type them as well as the cell's contents or formula when you place the cursor on a cell.

- **Mouse Pointer** Indicates screen location mouse will affect. The pointer will change shape depending on the task performed. *(See MOUSE POINTER SHAPES, page xix.)*

(continued...)

xviii

WINDOW SCREEN PARTS DESCRIPTION (continued)

- **SmartIcons** — Represent commonly used commands and macros.

- **Status Indicator** — Indicates status of the keyboard, worksheet or macro performance.

Release 4 Worksheet Screen

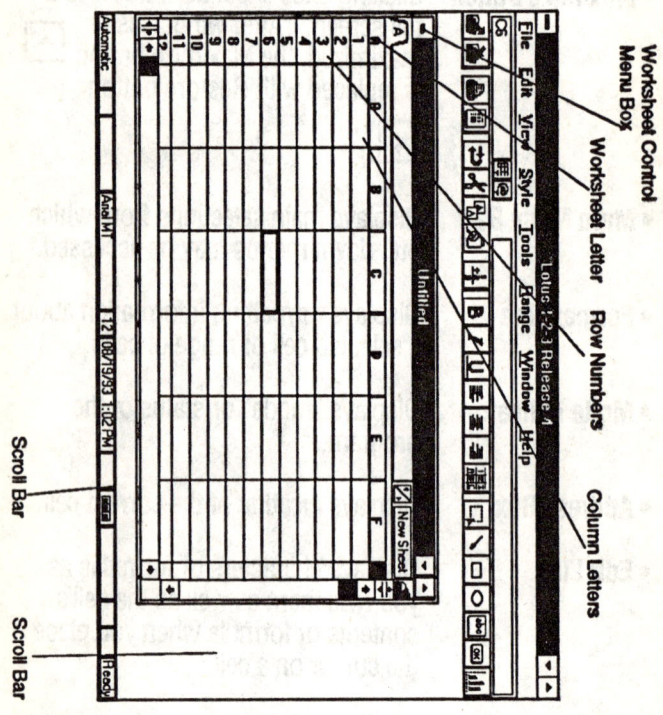

(continued...)

WINDOW SCREEN PARTS DESCRIPTION (continued)

- **Worksheet Control Menu Box**   Double clicking will close worksheet file; clicking once will access a pull-down menu.

- **Worksheet Letter**   Identifies each of the 256 possible worksheets in a worksheet file.

- **Column Letters/ Row Numbers**   Comprises worksheet frame.

- **Scroll Bars**   Click these arrows to view other parts of worksheet.

Mouse Terminology

> *NOTE:*   *Use the left mouse button unless otherwise noted.*

Mouse Pointer   As mouse moves, pointer ⇖ moves to indicate screen location. (The mouse pointer will change its shape depending on the task you perform. *[See **MOUSE POINTER SHAPES**, page 182).*

Click   Quickly press and release mouse button.

Double Click   Press mouse button twice in rapid succession.

Drag   Press and hold mouse button while moving the mouse.

(continued...)

Procedure Terminology

Highlight or   Drag mouse until desired range is
Select Range   highlighted; then release mouse
                        button.

Select   Point to desired item and click once.

ACCESSING COMMANDS ("Classic" menu)

Press the / or : key to access "Classic" commands and
"WYSIWYG menus"; then, use the arrow keys and Enter, or
press the first character in each item to access selections.
The mouse does not work in this window. The menu
structure matches that used in releases 3 and 3.1. Classic
menu keystrokes are indicated at the beginning of
procedures.

Using the Menu Bar

Use mouse to point to a menu bar item and click once.

OR

Use the keyboard to access a menu bar item (press Alt +
underlined letter on menu item). Note the main menu bar:

<u>F</u>ile	<u>E</u>dit	<u>V</u>iew	<u>S</u>tyle	<u>T</u>ools	<u>R</u>ange	<u>W</u>indow	<u>H</u>elp

*After menu is selected from the main menu, a **pull-down**
menu appears listing commands. These selections may
also be accessed using the mouse or Alt and the
underlined letter.*

(continued...)

USING THE MENU BAR (continued)

NOTE: *The pull-down menu which appears after selecting Tools from the menu bar:*

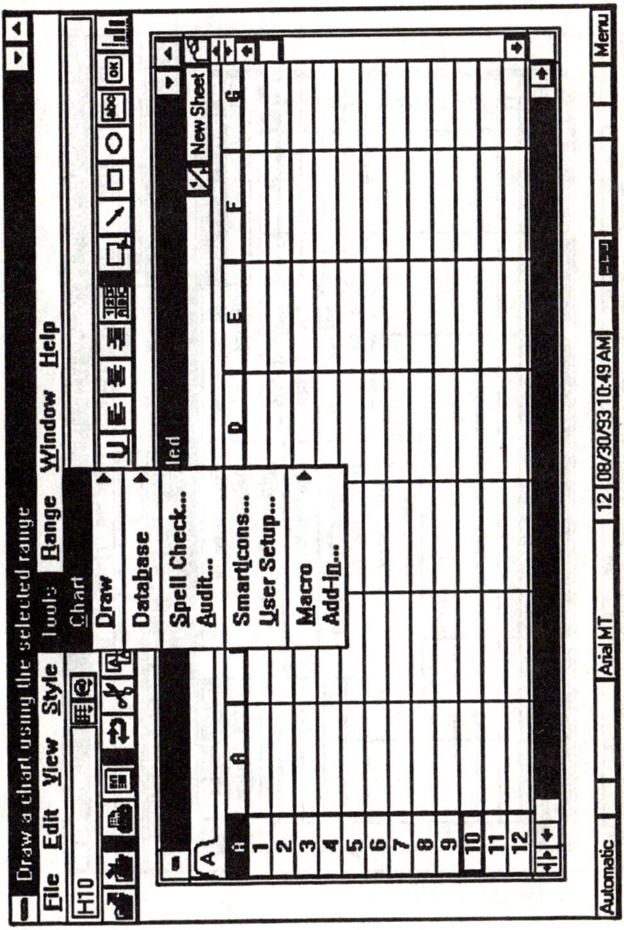

(continued...)

xxii

USING THE MENU BAR (continued)

Pull-down menu items with an arrowhead following the word indicate a cascade menu follows. A **cascade** menu is a submenu of the selection. Note the cascade menu which follows the Database selection:

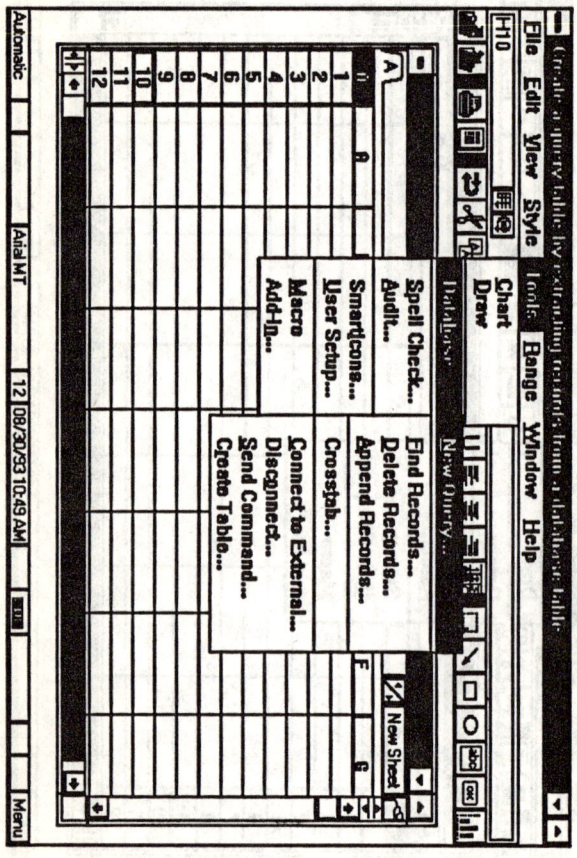

(continued...)

USING THE MENU BAR (continued)

Pull-down menu items with an ellipsis (...) following the
word indicate a dialog box follows. A **dialog box** asks for
additional information to complete a task. Note dialog
box below:

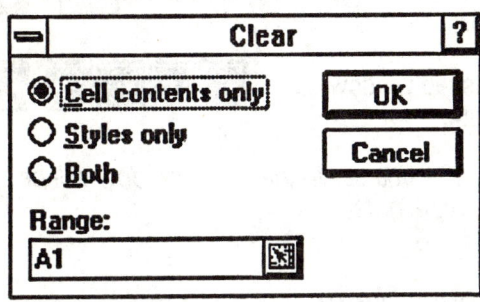

NOTE: *A menu item or dialog box may contain
"grayed" or "dimmed" items. These
items are not available at this time.*

Get Help

To access Help:

Select **Help** on main menu bar.

OR

Press **F1** F1

(See HELP, page 71.)

MANAGE WINDOWS

Activate Window

Click anywhere in desired window.

OR

1. Click **Window** .... `Alt` + `W`
   in menu.

2. Click desired window .... `↑` `↓` `←` `→` , `↵`
   to activate.

   *NOTE: The title bar in the active window will be
   highlighted.*

Open Control Menu

1. Click **Control box** `▬` .... `Alt` + `-`
   of desired window (located in
   the top left corner of any window).

2. Click desired item .... `↑` `↓` , `↵`

There are two types of windows: **application** and
document. Lotus worksheets are displayed in document
windows. Use the **Next** command in the Control menu to
move among the worksheets open on the screen
concurrently.

Maximize Window

Click **Maximize button** ▲ of desired window (located in top right corner of specified window).

OR

1. Click **Control box** ▭ .... **Alt** + **-**

2. Click **Maximize**... **X**

> *NOTE: The Restore button [insert graphic]
> replaces the Maximize button after
> window is maximized.*

Restore Window

Click **Restore** button ⬍ of desired window (located in top right corner of specified window).

OR

1. Click **Control box** ▭ .... **Alt** + **-**

2. Click **Restore**... **R**

Minimize Window

Click **Minimize** button ▼ of desired window (located in top right corner of the specified window).

OR

1. Click **Control box** ▭ .... **Alt** + **-**

2. Click **Minimize** .... **N**

xxvi

Restore Minimized Window

Double click desired window icon to restore.

OR

1. Click **Control box** ⊟ .... Alt + ▬

2. Click **Restore** .... R

Change Size of Window

1. Position mouse pointer on any border or corner of window until double-headed arrow appears.

2. Click and drag mouse until window is desired size.

3. Release mouse button.

OR

1. Click **Control box** ⊟ .... Alt + ▬

2. Click **Size** .... Z

3. Press **Enter** .... ↵

4. Press arrow keys .... ↑ ↓ ← →
   to size window.

5. Press **Enter** .... ↵

Move Window

1. Position mouse pointer on desired window of title bar.

2. Click and drag mouse to move window to new location.

3. Release mouse button.

OR

1. Click **Control box** ⬜ .... `Alt` + `-`

2. Click **M**ove.. `M`

3. Press **Enter**... `←┘`

4. Press arrow keys........................... `↑` `↓` `←` `→`
   to move window.

5. Press **Enter**... `←┘`

Cascade Windows

1. Click **W**indow.................................... `Alt` + `W`

2. Click **C**ascade .... `C`

   NOTE: *The active window will always be "on top"*
   of the others.

Tile Windows

1. Click **W**indow.................................... `Alt` + `W`

2. Click **T**ile... `T`

xxviii

Close Window

Double click **Control Menu** box `[—]` (located in top left corner of window).

OR

Press **Ctrl+F4** .... `Ctrl` + `F4`
to close window.

OR

1. Click **Control box** `[—]` .... `Alt` + `-`

2. Click **Close** .... `C`

3. Press **Enter** .... `⏎`

Exit Windows

1. Click **File** .... `Alt` + `F`

2. Click **Exit windows** .... `X`

3. Click **OK** .... `⏎`

APPLICATION PROGRAMS

Load

-Classic keystrokes-

Alt F10 , L , highlight program, ⏎ , N or 1 or 2 or 3

1. Click **T**ools .... Alt + T

2. Click **Add-i**n .... N

3. Click file to be loaded.

4. Click **L**oad .... Alt + L

Invoke

-Classic keystrokes-

Alt F10 , I , highlight program, ⏎

Remove

-Classic keystrokes-

Alt F10 , R , highlight program, ⏎

1. Click **T**ools .... Alt + T

2. Click **Add-i**n .... N

3. Click file to be removed.

4. Click **R**emove .... Alt + R

2

Clear

Removes all add-ins from memory for current work session.

-Classic keystrokes-

1. Click **T**ool .... Alt + T
2. Click **Add-i**n .... N
3. Click **Remove A**ll .... Alt + A

Create Table of Add-in Programs

-Classic keystrokes-

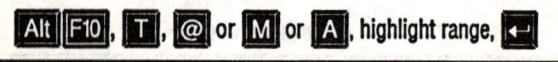

AUDIT

Finds and analyzes formulas. Also, locates circular references and DDE and file links. In general, Audit is useful when examining a worksheet. For example, Audit can discover the source of errors and see if a range you want to delete is used in any formula.

To use the Audit feature you must know three things:

1. *What you want to find. The options are:*

   - *All formulas in the worksheet*

   - *Formula precedents in the worksheet*

   - *Formula dependents in the worksheet*

   - *File links*

   - *DDE links*

2. *How you want the results displayed. The options are selecting all cells of the type you specify, or creating a list.*

3. *What you want to audit. You can audit either the current file or formulas in all active files.*

Find Formulas

1. Click **T**ools .... Alt + T

2. Click **A**udit .... A

3. Click **A**ll formulas .... A
   under **Audit**.

(continued...)

4

FIND FORMULAS (continued)

4. Choose one of the following under **Produce a** section of dialog box:

   Selection.................................... `Alt` + `S`
   to select cells.

   OR

   a. **Report at range**.................... `Alt` + `R`
      to display list of cells.

   b. Type a blank range in text box..............*range*

5. Choose one of the following under **Limit audit to** section of dialog box:

   • **Current file**................................ `Alt` + `U`
     to search all worksheets
     in the current file.

   • **All files**.................................... `Alt` + `I`
     to search for worksheets
     in all active files.

   *NOTE: The All files option is only available if
   Report at range option was selected in
   step 4.*

6. Click **OK**... `↵`

Find Precedents/Dependents

*Formula precedents are cells referred to by formula. Cell
dependents are cells containing formulas that refer to
data in a range.*

1. Highlight (select) range whose precedents/dependents
   you want to find.

(continued...)

FIND PRECEDENTS/DEPENDENTS (continued)

2. Click **T**ools .... `Alt` + `T`

3. Click **A**udit .... `A`

4. Choose one of the following:

   • Formula **p**recedents .... `Alt` + `P`

   • Cell **d**ependents .... `Alt` + `D`

5. Choose one of the following under **Produce a** section of dialog box:

   Selection .... `Alt` + `S`
   to select cells.

   OR

   a. **R**eport at range .... `Alt` + `R`
      to display list of cells.

   b. Type a blank range in text box ....*range*

6. Choose one of the following under **Limit audit to** section of dialog box:

   • C**u**rrent file .... `Alt` + `U`
     to search all worksheets
     in current file.

   • All f**i**les .... `Alt` + `I`
     to search for worksheets
     in all active files.

   NOTE: *The All files option is only available if*
   Report at range option was selected in
   step 5.

7. Click **OK** .... `↵`

6

Find Circular Reference

A circular reference is a formula that refers directly (or indirectly) to itself.

1. Click **T**ools .... `Alt` + `T`

2. Click **A**udit .... `A`

3. Click **C**ircular references .... `C`
   under Audit.

4. Choose one of the following under **Produce a** section
   of dialog box:

   Selection .... `Alt` + `S`
   to select cells.

   OR

   a. **R**eport at range .... `Alt` + `R`
      to display list of cells.

   b. Type a blank range in text box .... *range*

5. Choose one of the following under **Limit audit to**
   section of dialog box:

   - **C**urrent file .... `Alt` + `U`
     to search all worksheets
     in current file.

   - **A**ll f**i**les .... `Alt` + `I`
     to search for worksheets
     in all active files.

   NOTE: *The All files option is only available if*
   Report at range option was selected in
   step 4.

6. Click **OK** .... `⏎`

Find Links

*Audit can find two different types of links: file and DDE. A **file link** is a formula that refers to data in other 1-2-3 files. A **DDE link** is a link between a 1-2-3 file and another Windows application.*

1. Highlight (select) range whose precedents/dependents you want to find.

2. Click **T**ools .... `Alt` + `T`

3. Click **A**udit .... `A`

4. Choose one of the following under **Audit:**

    *   **F**ile links................................. `Alt` + `F`

    *   DD**E** links................................. `Alt` + `E`

5. Choose one of the following under **Produce a** section of dialog box:

    Selection...................................... `Alt` + `S`
    to select cells.

    OR

    a. **R**eport at range....................... `Alt` + `R`
        to display list of cells.

    b. Type a blank range in text box..............*range*

6. Choose one of the following under **Limit audit to** section of dialog box:

    *   **C**urrent file.............................. `Alt` + `U`
        to search all worksheets
        in current file.

(continued...)

FIND LINKS (continued)

- **All files**...⬛Alt + ⬛I
to search for worksheets
in all active files.

> *NOTE:* *The All files option is only available if*
> *Report at range option was selected in*
> *step 5.*

7. Click **OK** ....⬛↵

BACKSOLVER

Allows you to perform "backward" what-if problems to
achieve a result from a formula cell.

Select BackSolver Options

Use Undo to return the adjustable cell to the original
value using BackSolver.

1. Click **R**ange....................................⬛Alt + ⬛R

2. Click **A**nalyze..⬛A

3. Click **B**ackSolver...⬛B

4. Type cell address containing formula in **Make cell** box.
(Identifies cell containing formula in the worksheet.)

5. Click **E**qual to value box.......................⬛Alt + ⬛E

6. Type value...*number*
(Identifies value in worksheet
that cell is to equal.)

7. Click **B**y changing cell(s) box ....⬛Alt + ⬛B

(continued...)

SELECT BACKSOLVER OPTIONS (continued)

8. Type **By changing cell(s)**. (Identifies cell where result should appear.)

9. Click **OK** .... ⏎

CANCEL COMMAND

Click **Cancel** .... Esc

OR

Press **Esc** .... Esc
to backup one menu level
or command step at a time.

OR

Press **Ctrl+Break** .... Ctrl + Break
to completely stop a procedure.

CHANGE APPEARANCE OF DATA

Classic keystrokes are only available for alignment.

Lineup Typeface

A typeface is the design of a character.

1. Highlight range to receive font set change.

2. Click **Style** .... Alt + S

3. Click **Font & Attributes** .... F

4. Click font name .... ⏎

5. Click **OK** .... ⏎

10

Lineup Typestyle

A typestyle is the treatment of characters for emphasis, such as bold, italic or underline. Ranges may also be colored (for color monitors and printers).

1. Highlight range to receive typestyle change.

2. Click **S**tyle .... `Alt` + `S`

3. Click **F**ont & Attributes .... `F`

4. Choose one of the following:

   • **B**old .... `Alt` + `B`

   • **N**ormal .... `Alt` + `N`

   • **I**talic .... `Alt` + `I`

   • **U**nderline .... `Alt` + `U` , `↑` `↓`
     (select underline
     type).

5. Click **OK** .... `↵`

Color and Pattern

1. Highlight range to receive color change.

2. Click **S**tyle .... `Alt` + `S`

3. Click **L**ines & Color .... `L`

   To change background color:

   a. Click **Background color** .... `Alt` + `B`

   b. Click desired color.

(continued...)

COLOR AND PATTERN (continued)

To change pattern:

a. Click **P**attern box...................... `Alt` + `P`

b. Click desired pattern.

To change pattern and color:

a. Click **Pattern & c**olor............... `Alt` + `C`

b. Click desired pattern.

To change text color:

a. Click **Te**x**t color**...................... `Alt` + `X`

b. Click desired color.

To display negative values in red:

Click **negative v**alues **in red**......... `Alt` + `V`

4. Click **OK** .... `↵`

Borders and Frames

Adds lines along the edges of cells in a range. Entire ranges or cells can be outlined.

1. Highlight range to receive border change.

2. Click **S**tyle .... `Alt` + `S`

3. Click **L**ines **& Color** .... `L`

(continued...)

BORDERS AND FRAMES (continued)

4. Select border option:

- **Outline** .... Alt + O
  to draw line around outside edge
  of current selection.

- **All** .... Alt + L
  to draw line along all edges
  of each cell.

- **Left** .... Alt + E
  to draw line along left edge
  of each cell.

- **Top** .... Alt + T
  to draw line along top edge
  of each cell.

- **Right** .... Alt + R
  to draw line along right edge
  of each cell.

- **Bottom** .... Alt + M
  to draw line along bottom edge
  of each cell.

5. Select a line style:

   a. Click line box next to border setting.

   b. Click **Line style** .... Alt + Y

   c. Click desired style.

(continued...)

BORDERS AND FRAMES (continued)

6. Select a line color:

    a. Click line box next to border setting.

    b. Click **Li_ne color** .... Alt + N

    c. Click desired color.

7. Select collections and ranges for cell:

    a. Click **Designer frame** .... Alt + D
        drop-down box.

    b. Click desired frame.

    c. Click **Frame color** .... Alt + F
        drop-down box.

    d. Click desired color.

Alignment

-Classic keystrokes-

1. Highlight range to be aligned.

2. Click **S_tyle** .... Alt + S

3. Click **Alignment** .... A

(continued...)

ALIGNMENT (continued)

4. Select horizontal alignment option:

    - L̲eft .... `Alt` + `L`

    - C̲enter .... `Alt` + `C`

    - R̲ight... `Alt` + `R`

    - E̲venly spaced.......................... `Alt` + `E`

    - Acr̲oss columns .... `Alt` + `O`

5. Click **OK** .... `↵`

Lines

Allows you to change styles for lines drawn with the Draw Lines command in Graph Mode.

CHANGE SCREEN DISPLAY OPTIONS

> *NOTE:* *Changing the way a worksheet appears on the screen does not affect the printed worksheet or graphics.*

Set Preferences

1. Click V̲iew.. `Alt` + `V`

2. Click **Set View P̲references** .... `P`

(continued...)

SET PREFERENCES (continued)

3. Choose one or more of the following options under **Show** in current file:

- Worksheet frame.................. `Alt` + `W`
- Worksheet tabs .... `Alt` + `T`
- Grid lines .... `Alt` + `G`
- Scroll bars .... `Alt` + `S`
- Page breaks....................... `Alt` + `P`
- Charts, drawings and pictures........................ `Alt` + `C`

4. Select frame from drop down box, if desired.

5. Select color of grid lines from drop down box, if desired.

6. Enter new size in **Custom zoom %** to change default display size of cells.

7. Choose one or more of the following options under **Show in 1-2-3**:

- SmartIcons .... `Alt` + `I`
- Edit line............................. `Alt` + `E`
- Status bar .... `Alt` + `B`

NOTE: *These selections become the default settings for all files in memory and new files. To change the default settings for one worksheet, use Style Worksheet Defaults command.*

8. Click **OK** .... `⏎`

Show Frame, Grid Lines, Drawn Objects

1. Click **F**ile .... `Alt` + `F`

2. Click **Page Setup** .... `G`

3. Choose one or more of the following under **Show:**

   • Wor**k**sheet frame .... `Alt` + `K`

   • **G**rid lines .... `Alt` + `G`

   • Drawn **o**bjects .... `Alt` + `O`

4. Click **OK** .... `⏎`

Zoom Worksheet

Shrinks/magnifies display of worksheet by 10%.

1. Click **V**iew .... `Alt` + `V`

2. Choose one of the following options:

   • **Z**oom In.. `Z`

   • Zoom **O**ut .... `O`

Reset Cell Size

Returns cells to default size.

1. Click **V**iew .... `Alt` + `V`

2. Click **C**ustom .... `C`

Change Color/Pattern

1. Highlight (select) range or collection you wish to change.

2. Click **S**tyle .... `Alt` + `S`

(continued...)

CHANGE COLOR/PATTERN (continued)

3. Click **Lines & Color**....................................... L

   To change data color:

   Select color in **Text** drop-down box.

   To change background color:

   Select color in **Background color** drop-down box.

   To display negative values in red:

   Select **Negative values in red** ...... Alt + V

   To change background pattern:

   Select pattern in **Pattern** drop-down box.

   To change color of background pattern:

   Select color from **Pattern color** drop-down box.

4. Click **OK** .... ⏎

CHANGE DIRECTORY

Overrides the default directory for the current session.

-Classic keystrokes-

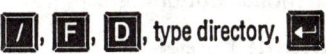
/ , F , D , type directory, ⏎

18

CHART

Lotus 1-2-3 Release 4 for Windows offers the following types of charts: Area, Bar (e.g., Comparison Bar, Horizontal Bar, Horizontal Stacked Bar, Vertical Bar, Vertical Stacked Bar), HLCO, Line, Mixed, Pie, Radar (also Filled Radar), 3D Area, 3D Area Depth, 3D Bar, 3D Line, 3D Pie, 3D Vertical Bar and XY.

Create Chart

> *NOTE: When you create a chart, 1-2-3 uses the default type.*

1. Highlight (select) range or collection you wish to chart.

2. Click **T**ools .... `Alt` + `T`

3. Click **C**hart .... `C`

The mouse pointer changes to the shape of a chart.

To create chart in default size:

Click worksheet where you want upper left corner.

To size chart to your specifications:

a. Position cursor where you want upper left corner.

b. Hold down mouse button and drag right and down until outline is desired size.

c. Release mouse button.

Change Default Chart

1. Create chart using the previous procedure.

2. Change chart type using next procedure.

3. Click **C**hart .... `Alt` + `C`

CHANGE DEFAULT CHART (continued)

4. Click **S̲et Preferred**.. `S`

   *NOTE: After step 4, 1-2-3 uses the current type
   of chart as the default.*

Change Chart Type

1. Click (select) chart.

2. Click **C̲hart** .... `Alt` + `C`

3. Click **T̲ype**.. `T`

4. Click desired chart type under **Types.**

5. Click one of the following under **Orientation:**

   • **Vertical**...................................... `Alt` + `V`
     to display x-axis
     across bottom of chart.

   • **Horizontal** .... `Alt` + `O`
     to display x-axis
     along left edge of chart.

   **If you moved the chart and want to return it to
   default location:**

   Click under **Placement.**

(Re)Name Chart

*1-2-3 automatically assigns a name to any chart you
create (e.g., Chart1). Use this procedure to change the
name assigned by 1-2-3. You can then use the **Find**
Chart procedure (below), to find the chart easily.*

1. Highlight (select) chart.

(continued...)

(RE)NAME CHART (continued)

2. Click **Chart** .... `Alt` + `C`

3. Click **Name** .... `N`

4. Type chart name.......................................*name*

5. Click **Rename** .... `Alt` + `R`

Find Chart

1. Click **Edit**... `Alt` + `E`

2. Click **Go To** .... `G`

3. Highlight chart in **Type of item** drop down box.

   NOTE: Highlight the file name (in the In file drop-down box) if the chart is in another active file.

4. Highlight (select) chart name.

5. Click **OK** .... `↵`

CHART ENHANCEMENTS

NOTE: Many of the procedures to reposition parts of a chart have a Manual option. This choice indicates you have previously dragged that part of the chart (e.g., title) to the desired location.

Change All Legend Labels

1. Highlight (select) chart.

(continued...)

CHANGE ALL LEGEND LABELS (continued)

2. Double click the legend.

    OR

    a. Click **C**hart .... Alt + C

    b. Click **L**egend L

3. Highlight **[All ranges]** .... ↓ ↑ , ←
    in **Series** list box.

4. Type range .... *name* or *address*
    of cells containing text
    for legends in the **Legend
    entry** box.

    To change location:

    Choose one of the following under **Place:**

    • **R**ight of plot .... Alt + R

    • **B**elow plot .... Alt + B

    • **M**anual .... Alt + M

5. Click **OK** .... ←

Change Individual Legend Labels

1. Highlight (select) chart.

2. Double click the legend.

    OR

    a. Click **C**hart .... Alt + C

    b. Click **L**egend L

(continued...)

CHANGE INDIVIDUAL LEGEND LABELS (continued)

3. Highlight (select) a series .... ⬇️ ⬆️ , ↵
    in **Series list** box.

4. Type label ....*label*

    OR

    a. Click **C**ell .... Alt + C

    b. Type name or address ....*name* or *address*
        of cell containing text
        for legend.

    To change location:

    Choose one of the following under **Place**:

    •   **R**ight of plot.............................. Alt + R

    •   **B**elow plot.................................. Alt + B

    •   **M**anual.. Alt + M

5. Click **OK** .... ↵

Add Titles/Notes

1. Highlight (select) chart.

2. Click **C**hart .... Alt + C

3. Click **H**eadings .... H

    To type title:

    Type title in **Line 1** text box, and subtitle in **Line 2**
    text box under **Title**.

(continued...)

ADD TITLES/NOTES (continued)

To use title in cell(s):

a. Click **Cell** check box under **Title**.

b. Type cell location for title in **Line 1** text box.

c. Repeat step a.

d. Type cell location for subtitle in **Line 2** text box.

4. Repeat step 3, under **Footnote,** for note(s).

5. Click **OK** .... ⏎

Move Titles/Notes

The quickest way to move a title or note is to drag it to the new location.

1. Highlight (select) chart.

2. Double click title or note.

   OR

   a. Click **C**hart .... Alt + C

   b. Click **H**eadings .... H

3. Select Left, Center or Right under **Title** or **Footnote**.

   NOTE: *If you have previously dragged the title or note, select Manual.*

4. Click **OK** .... ⏎

Explode Pie Slices

The easiest way to explode a pie slice is to drag it.

> *NOTE: To change the color of a pie slice, highlight it and use the Style Lines & Color command.*

1. Highlight (select) chart

2. Click **Chart** .... `Alt` + `C`

3. Click **D**ata Labels .... `D`

4. a. Click **A**ll by .... `Alt` + `A`

   b. Click arrows .... `↑` `↓` `→` `←`

   OR

   Type percentage .... *percentage*

5. Click **OK** .... `↵`

Change Axis Title

1. Double click axis title.

   OR

   a. Click **C**hart .... `Alt` + `C`

   b. Click **A**xis .... `A`

   c. Choose one of the following:

   - **X**-Axis .... `X`

   - **Y**-Axis .... `Y`

   - **2**nd Y-Axis .... `2`

(continued...)

CHANGE AXIS TITLE (continued)

To create new title:

Type title in **Axis title** text box ....*title*

To use title in cell(s):

a. Click **Cell** check box, under **Axis title**.

b. Type cell location for title in **Axis title** text box.

2. Click **OK** .... ⏎

Add/Change Units Title

Changes the scale for each axis.

1. Double click axis title.

    OR

    a. Click **C**hart .... Alt + C

    b. Click **A**xis .... A

    c. Choose one of the following:

    • **X**-Axis.................................... X

    • **Y**-Axis.................................... Y

    • **2**nd Y-Axis.............................. 2

2. Click **O**ptions................................. Alt + O

    NOTE: If a chart has a units title, double click the title to display the Options dialog box.

(continued...)

ADD/CHANGE UNITS TITLE (continued)

3. Do one of the following under **Units title:**

   Click **A**utomatic .... `Alt` + `A`

   OR

   a. Click **M**anual .... `Alt` + `M`

   b. Type type title in text box.

      OR

      i. Click **Cell**.

      ii. Type cell address .... *address*

4. Click **OK** .... `↵`

Set Tick Marks/Axis Labels

Tick marks show the scale of a chart. Axis labels identify the tick marks.

1. Highlight (select) chart.

   OR

   a. Click **C**hart .... `Alt` + `C`

   b. Click **A**xis .... `A`

   c. Choose one of the following:

      • **X**-Axis .... `X`

      • **Y**-Axis .... `Y`

      • **2**nd Y-Axis .... `2`

(continued...)

SET TICK MARKS/AXIS LABELS (continued)

2. Select one or both of the following under **Show tick marks at:**

   - Major interval .... $\boxed{\text{Alt}}$ + $\boxed{\text{A}}$
   - Minor interval .... $\boxed{\text{Alt}}$ + $\boxed{\text{V}}$

   NOTE: If axis labels are values in your chart, you can use the Style Number Format command to change their format without changing the format of the data in the worksheet.

3. Click arrows................................. $\boxed{\uparrow}$ $\boxed{\downarrow}$ $\boxed{\rightarrow}$ $\boxed{\leftarrow}$

   OR

   Enter number in text box in **Place label every.**

4. Click **OK** .... $\boxed{\leftarrow}$

Change Axis Scale

When you create a chart, 1-2-3 automatically sets the scale of the axes. A numerical axis can be changed to the following:

- *A linear or standard scale (numbers increase or decrease in fixed units).*

- *A log scale (numbers increase or decrease log arithmetically).*

- *A 100% scale (numbers range from 0% to 100%).*

You can also change the upper and lower limits of the scale.

Set Scale Manually

1. Double click the axis you wish to change.

   OR

   a. Highlight (select) chart.

   b. Click **Chart**..................................... `Alt` + `C`

   c. Click **Axis** .... `A`

   d. Choose one of the following:

   - **X**-Axis.. `X`

   - **Y**-Axis.. `Y`

   - **2**nd Y-Axis...................................... `2`

   To change scale type:

   a. Click **Options** .... `Alt` + `O`

   b. Select desired option from **Type of scale** drop-down box.

   c. Click **OK**.. `←`

   To create scale within certain upper and lower limits:

   a. Type upper limit in **Upper limit** text box under **Scale manually.**

   b. Type lower limit in **Lower limit** text box under **Scale manually.**

   NOTE: If upper limit is lower than the lower limit, a blank rectangle displays instead of a chart.

(continued...)

SET SCALE MANUALLY (continued)

To change intervals between tick marks:

a. Type major interval in **Major interval** text box under **Scale manually.**

b. Type minor interval in **Minor interval** text box under **Scale manually.**

2. Click **OK** .... ⏎

Display Values, Percentages, Labels/Non-Pie

Creates labels from data in worksheet range(s).

1. Highlight (select) chart.

2. Click **Chart** .... Alt + C

3. Click **Data Labels** .... D

4. Highlight data series in **Series list** box.

OR

Click **All ranges** .... Alt + A

5. Indicate the range containing the information you want to use as data labels in the **Range of labels** text box.

When specifying a range, be aware of the following:

- *If you select a single data series in step 4, the range should be the same size as the data range.*

- *If you select **All ranges** in step 4, the range should be the same size as all data ranges combined.*

(continued...)

DISPLAY VALUES, PERCENTAGES, LABELS/NON-PIE (continued)

> • *If you want to label only some of the data series, leave the cells corresponding to the values you don't want to label blank.*

6. Select a position for labels (e.g., Center, Right, Below, Left, Above) from the **Placement** drop-down box.

   NOTE: For stacked bars, the default position is inside corresponding parts of bars. For cluster bars, the default position is above.

7. Click **OK** .... ⏎

Display Values, Percentages, Labels/Pie

1. Highlight (select) chart.

2. Click **Chart** .... Alt + C

3. Click **Data Labels** .... D

4. Choose one or more of the following options under **Show:**

   • **Values** .... Alt + V

   • **Percentages** .... Alt + P

   • **Contents of X data range** .... Alt + C
     displays label
     for each pie slice.

   • **Hide/show percent
     using C range** .... Alt + H
     shows percentages of slices
     using worksheet range.

5. Click **OK** .... ⏎

CLOSE FILE

1. Click **F**ile .... `Alt` + `F`

2. Click **C**lose .... `C`

3. Choose one of the following options:

    *   **Y**es .... `Y`

    *   **N**o .... `N`

    *   Cancel .... `Esc`

COLUMN WIDTH AND ROW HEIGHT

The column width default is 9 characters. 1-2-3 measures row height in points. The row height default is 14 points. 1-2-3 will automatically adjust the height of a row to accommodate the largest font size in a row.

Change Columns to Specified Width

1. Select range that includes cells in columns you wish to change.

2. Click **S**tyle .... `Alt` + `S`

3. Click **C**olumn Width .... `C`

    To change width:

    a. Click **S**et width to .... `Alt` + `S`

    b. Click arrows or type width from 1-240 characters.

    To adjust each column to width of widest entry:

    Click **F**it widest entry .... `Alt` + `F`

(continued...)

CHANGE COLUMNS TO SPECIFIED WIDTH (continued)

To reset to width defined in Style Worksheet Defaults:

Click <u>R</u>eset to worksheet
default.. `Alt` + `R`

4. Click **OK** .... `↵`

Single Column/Dragging

When a value is too wide for a cell, it will appear either in scientific notation or as a line of asterisks (****). To display the value, widen the column.

1. Move mouse pointer to letter of column you want to change.

2. Point to right column border.

The mouse pointer changes to a black, two-headed horizontal arrow.

3. Drag left to narrow column. Drag right to widen it.

4. Release mouse button when column is desired width.

Multiple Columns/Dragging

1. Highlight (select) entire column where the cells reside. (Select column letters.)

2. Point to border between any of the column letters in highlighted columns.

The mouse pointer changes to a black, two-headed horizontal arrow.

3. Drag left to narrow column or drag right to widen it.

4. Release mouse button when column is desired width.

> *NOTE: 1-2-3 changes width of all selected columns to match the one you dragged.*

Change Rows to Specified Height

1. Select range that includes cells in rows to be changed.

2. Click **Style** .... `Alt` + `S`

3. Click **Row Height** .... `R`

    To change height:

    a. Click **Set height to** .... `Alt` + `S`

    b. Click arrows or type height from 1-255 points.

    NOTE: When row height is adjusted to number of points, it no longer automatically adjusts to fit largest font in row.

    To reset height of each row to height of largest font:

    Click **Fit largest font** .... `Alt` + `F`

4. Click **OK** .... `↵`

Change Single Row/Dragging

1. Move mouse pointer to number of row you want to change.

2. Point to lower border of row.

The mouse pointer changes to a black, two-headed vertical arrow.

3. Drag up to narrow row. Drag down to widen it.

4. Release mouse button when row is desired height.

Change Multiple Rows/Dragging

1. Highlight (select) entire column where the cell resides. (Select column letters.)

2. Point to border between any of the row numbers in highlighted rows.

The mouse pointer changes to a black, two-headed vertical arrow.

3. Drag up to narrow row. Drag down to widen it.

4. Release mouse button when row is desired height.

> NOTE: *1-2-3 changes height of all selected rows to match the one you dragged.*

COMBINE FILES

1. Place cursor on cell where combined data is to begin.

2. Click **File** .... `Alt` + `F`

3. Click **Open** .... `O`

4. Type file name ....*filename*

5. Click **Combine** .... `Alt` + `C`

6. Click **Entire** file .... `Alt` + `E`
   under **Read.**

   OR

   a. Click **Range** .... `Alt` + `R`

   b. Type range ....*range*

(continued...)

COMBINE FILES (continued)

7. Do one of the following under **Effect** in current file:

    To copy specified data from file on disk to current file:

    Click **Replace value** .... `Alt` + `V`

    NOTE: Blank cells from file on disk will not replace blank cells in the current file.

    To add numeric data from file on disk to current file:

    Click **Add to values** .... `Alt` + `A`

    NOTE: This procedure works with numeric data only. Do not use this option to add date or time numbers.

    To subtract numeric data from file on disk from current file:

    Click **Subtract from values** .... `Alt` + `S`

    NOTE: This procedure works with numeric data only. Do not use this option to add date or time numbers.

8. Click **OK** .... `↵`

COPY/PASTE

Copies a cell, range of cells or formula.

-Classic keystrokes-

position cursor in first cell to be copied from, **/**, **C**,

highlight FROM cell(s), **⏎**, position cursor in first cell to be

copied to, **.**, highlight TO cell(s), **⏎**

1. Highlight (select) cell or range to be copied.

2. Click **E**dit...**Alt** + **E**

3. Click **C**opy...**C**

   NOTE: Data will remain in Clipboard until new copy or cut is made.

4. Highlight (select) cell or range for copied data.

   NOTE: You only have to specify the top left cell. The range can be in the same file, another file or a different application. However, 1-2-3 will write over existing data.

5. Click **E**dit.......................................**Alt** + **E**

6. Click **P**aste...**P**

Copy with Drag and Drop

1. Highlight (select) range to be copied.

2. Move mouse pointer to edge of range, so it changes shape to a hand.

(continued...)

COPY WITH DRAG AND DROP (continued)

3. Hold down **Ctrl** and mouse button.

4. Drag range to new location.

5. Release **Ctrl** and mouse button when outline of range is in desired location.

Copy Range to Adjacent Cells

Use to copy top row or first column to remaining cells in range.

1. Highlight (select) range to be copied.

2. Click **E**dit .... Alt + E

    To copy first column of range to adjacent columns to the right:

    Click **Copy R**ight .... R

    To copy top row of range to adjacent rows below:

    Click **Copy Do**w**n** .... W

Copy Range of Values

Copies a range of data, replacing formulas with actual values. Only works with Classic keystrokes.

-Classic keystrokes-

position cursor in first cell to be copied from, / , R , V ,

highlight cell(s), ⏎ , position cursor in first cell to be copied to,

⏎

CREATE NEW FILE

| ☐ **/** , **F** , **N** , **B** or **A** , filename, **↵** |

1. Click **F**ile .... **Alt** + **F**

2. Click **N**ew .... **N**

CUT/PASTE

Moves a cell, range of cells or formula.

| Position cursor in first cell to be moved, **/** , **M** , highlight FROM cell(s), **↵** , position cursor in first cell to be moved to, **.** , highlight TO cell(s), **↵** |

1. Highlight (select) cell or range to be moved.

2. Click **E**dit .... **Alt** + **E**

3. Click **Cut** .... **T**

> *NOTE: Data will remain in Clipboard until new cut or copy is made.*

4. Highlight (select) cell or range for moved data.

> *NOTE: You only have to specify the top left cell. The range can be in the same file, another file or a different application. 1-2-3 will write over existing data, however.*

5. Click **E**dit .... **Alt** + **E**

6. Click **P**aste .... **P**

Cut/Paste with Drag and Drop

1. Highlight (select) range to be cut.

2. Move mouse pointer to edge of range, so it changes shape to a fist.

3. Hold down mouse button and drag range to new location.

4. Release mouse button when outline of range is in desired location.

DATA DISTRIBUTION

Use this feature to determine number of values falling into specific categories.

- **Values range**   Contains database of values to be categorized.

- **Bin range**   Contains categories of values to be counted (listed top to bottom, smallest to largest).

- **Frequency of results**   Entered in a blank area of cells to the right of the bin range.

NOTE: Only Classic keystrokes are available for this procedure.

-Classic keystrokes-

Position cursor at top of empty column (adjacent to last column of data), type bin range (ascending order), **/** , **d** , **d** , highlight values in frequency distribution, **↵** , highlight bin range, **↵**

NOTE: Frequency will appear in column to the right of the bin range.

DATA FILL

Use the procedures in this section to have 1-2-3 automatically type numbers, dates, days, months and times into a worksheet. There are two different ways to have 1-2-3 fill in information on a worksheet. You can specify all the information 1-2-3 needs (Range Fill) or you can type an example and have 1-2-3 do the work, based on your example (Fill by Example).

Range Fill

-Classic keystrokes-

position cursor, `/`, `D`, `F` , highlight range, `⏎`, type start value, `⏎`, type step value, `⏎`, type stop value, `⏎`

1. Highlight (select) range to be filled.

2. Click **R**ange... `Alt` + `R`

3. Click **F**ill .... `F`

To change start number:

a. Position cursor in **S**tart............ `Alt` + `S`

b. Type starting number (e.g., 5) ...*startnumber*

To change increment:

a. Position cursor in **I**ncrement... `Alt` + `I`

b. Type number ....*incrementnumber* by which you want to increment (e.g., 5).

(continued...)

RANGE FILL (continued)

To change stop:

a. Position cursor in **S**top .... `Alt` + `S`

b. Type ending number .... *stopnumber* (e.g., 100).

To change interval options:

Choose one of the following:

- **L**inear .... `L`

- **Y**ear .... `Y`

- **Q**uarter .... `Q`

- **M**onth .... `M`

- **W**eek .... `W`

- **D**ay .... `D`

- **H**our .... `H`

- Mi**n**ute .... `N`

- Se**c**ond .... `C`

To change range to be filled:

a. Click **R**ange .... `Alt` + `R`

b. Type new fill range .... *fill range*

4. Click **OK** .... `↵`

Range Fill by Example

1. Type the first one or two cells in your range.

    *NOTE: If you want 1-2-3 to fill in single
    increments, you only need one cell (e.g.,
    1, January, A, etc.). If you want 1-2-3 to
    fill in more than single increments,
    however, you need two cells (e.g., 2,4 or
    January, March or A, C, etc.). 1-2-3 will
    then determine the increment you want by
    the increment between the first two cells.*

2. Highlight (select) entire range you want filled
    (including example cell(s)).

3. Click **R**ange.. Alt + R

4. Click **Fill by E**xample .... E

DATA PARSE

*After a file is imported, this procedure will separate long
labels into distinct text and numerical cell entries.*

-Classic keystrokes-

/ , D , P , F , C , I , highlight column, ← , O ,
highlight range, ← , G

1. Highlight (select) range to parse.

2. Click **R**ange.. Alt + R

3. Click **P**arse .... P

(continued...)

DATA PARSE (continued)

4. Click **C**reate .... Alt + C

5. Edit the format line, as needed.

6. Type range for parsed data in **O**utput Range.

   NOTE: Type either the first cell or the entire range.

7. Click **OK** .... ⏎

DATA QUERY

(See QUERY DATABASE, page 112.)

DATA REGRESSION

Use these procedures to determine if one set of data has a relationship to another.

Set Up Regression Analysis

1. Type values for y-range (dependent variables) in a column.

2. Type values for x-range (independent variables). The values for each variable must be in a separate column (e.g., Time, Temperature, etc.).

   NOTE: You may have from 1-75 independent variables. However, each column must have the same number of rows as the dependent variables column (see step 1). Also, the columns for independent variables must be adjacent to each other.

(continued...)

SET UP REGRESSION ANALYSIS (continued)

3. Choose an area in the worksheet where you want the results of the analysis displayed (output range).

   NOTE: 1-2-3 writes over all information in the output range.

Perform Regression Analysis

1. Click **R**ange .... `Alt` + `R`

2. Click **A**nalyze .... `A`

3. Click **R**egression .... `R`

   To specify X-range:

   a. Position cursor .... `Alt` + `X`
      in **X**-range box.

   b. Type X-range .... *x-range*

   To specify Y-range:

   a. Position cursor .... `Alt` + `Y`
      in **Y**-range box.

   b. Type Y-range .... *y-range*

   To specify Output range:

   a. Position cursor .... `Alt` + `O`
      in **O**utput range box.

   b. Type output range .... *outputrange*

(continued...)

PERFORM REGRESSION ANALYSIS (continued)

NOTE: Type a range 9 rows high and 4 columns wide, with an additional column for each independent variable after the second one. Or, specify only the upper left cell of an area that you know is available.

4. Click **Compute** .... `Alt` + `C`
to calculate values of y-intercept.

OR

Click **Set to zero** .... `Alt` + `Z`
to use zero as value
of the dependent variable
when independent variable is zero.

5. Click **Reset**.................................... `Alt` + `R`
to clear settings
and enter new ranges.

6. Click **OK**.. `↵`

DELETE CELL OR RANGE

(See ERASE, page 65.)

DELETE FILE

This feature works only with Classic keystrokes. You may, however, delete a file through Windows File Manager.

-Classic keystrokes-

`/`, `F`, `E`, `W` or `P` or `G` or `O`, highlight file,
`↵`, `Y` or `N`

46

DELETE WORKSHEET

-Classic keystrokes-

position cursor, ⬛**/**, ⬛**W**, ⬛**D**, ⬛**S**, ⬛**↵**

1. Position cursor on worksheet to be deleted.

   *NOTE: To delete worksheets B, C and D,
   highlight cells B:A1, C:A1 and D:A1.*

2. Click **E**dit .... **Alt** + **E**

3. Click **D**elete .... **D**

4. Click **S**heet .... **Alt** + **S**

5. Click **OK** .... **↵**

DRAWN OBJECTS

*Graphic items (e.g., arrow, drawing, rectangle, etc.) you
can add to a worksheet. Beside creating your own drawn
objects in 1-2-3, you can paste an object previously
copied or cut to the Clipboard. To paste in an object, use
the Edit Paste command.*

Create Arc, Arrow, Line

1. Click **T**ools .... **Alt** + **T**

2. Click **D**raw .... **D**

(continued...)

CREATE ARC, ARROW, LINE (continued)

3. Choose one of the following:

- Arc..C

- Arrow ....A

- Line L

4. Click mouse pointer where you want drawn object to begin.

5. Drag to where you want to end arc, arrow or line.

6. Release mouse button.

Create Ellipse or Rectangle

1. Click **Tools** ....Alt + T

2. Click **Draw** ....D

3. Choose one of the following:

- Ellipse..E

- Rectangle ....R

- Rounded Rectangle ....D

4. Click mouse pointer where you want drawn object to begin.

5. Drag to where you want to end ellipse or rectangle.

6. Release mouse button.

Create Freehand Drawing

1. Click **T**ools .... `Alt` + `T`

2. Click **D**raw .... `D`

3. Click **F**reehand .... `F`

4. Click mouse pointer where you want drawn object to begin.

5. Drag across worksheet.

6. Release mouse button.

Create Polygons or Polylines

1. Click **T**ools .... `Alt` + `T`

2. Click **D**raw .... `D`

3. Choose one of the following:

   • P**o**lyline .... `O`

   • **P**olygon .... `P`

4. Position mouse pointer where you want to draw first line.

   To draw straight line:

   Drag to where you want to end line.

   To draw freehand line:

   Hold down **Ctrl** and drag to where you want to end line.

5. Release mouse button.

6. Repeat step 4 to draw next line segment.

(continued...)

CREATE POLYGONS OR POLYLINES (continued)

7. Double click to end drawing.

> *NOTE:* *You do not need to draw the last line segment in a polygon. 1-2-3 automatically draws a line to connect the first line segment to the last line segment you draw.*

Create Text Block

1. Click Tools .... Alt + T

2. Click Draw .... D

3. Click Text .... T

To create default size text block:

Click where you would like top left-hand corner of text box to begin.

To create desired size:

Drag mouse pointer and release mouse button.

4. Type or paste text in text block ....*text*

> *NOTE:* *Text blocks can contain approximately 32,000 characters (about eight pages of text).*

5. Click the worksheet when you are done entering text.

Highlight (Select)/Size Drawn Object

1.   Position mouse pointer over object you want to select.

2.   Click object.

3.   Handles appear around object. Drag these handles to change object size, if desired.

Edit Text Block

1.   Highlight (select) text block.

2.   Double click text block.

3.   Edit text.

4.   Click the worksheet when you are done entering text.

Change Appearance of Text Block

Highlight (select) the text block to change the appearance of a text block. Then, use one of the following on the Style Menu: Alignment, Font & Attributes or Lines & Color.

> *NOTE: In a text block, you cannot use different fonts, attributes, etc. In other words, if you are going to make one word bold, you must make all words bold.*

Copy/Cut Drawn Object

*Highlight (select) the object as described above to copy or cut drawn objects. Then, use the Edit Copy or Edit Cut command. (See **COPY/PASTE**, page 36, and **CUT/PASTE**, page 38.)*

Delete Drawn Object

Highlight (select) the object as described above to delete a drawn object. Then, press Delete.

> NOTE: When you use Delete to remove a drawn object, the object is not automatically placed on the Clipboard. If you want to remove an object and reposition it somewhere else, use the Edit Cut command as described in the above procedure.

Change Line/Edge Color

Changes the width and style of lines in a drawn object.

1. Highlight (select) drawn object(s).

2. Click **Style** .... **Alt** + **S**

3. Click **Lines & Colors** .... **L**

4. Click desired style and width.

5. Click **OK** .... **↵**

Add Designer Frame

Can be added to charts, chart titles, legends, notes, rectangles, squares and text blocks. A designer frame can also include a drop shadow.

1. Highlight (select) object to be framed.

2. Click **Style** .... **Alt** + **S**

3. Click **Lines & Colors** .... **L**

4. Click desired frame in **Designer frame** drop-down box.

5. Click **OK** .... **↵**

Change Fill Pattern

Used for the interior of closed and solid drawn objects, pictures, shapes, etc. You can also make the fill pattern of an object transparent. When a drawn object has a transparent fill pattern, you can see through it.

1. Highlight (select) drawn object(s).

2. Click **S**tyle .... `Alt` + `S`

3. Click **L**ines & Colors .... `L`

4. Click desired frame in **Pattern** drop-down box.

5. Click **OK** .... `↵`

Change Background/Pattern Color

*When using a fill pattern in an object, you can choose two different colors: background and pattern. **Background color** is the color inside the object, behind the pattern. **Pattern color** is the color of the pattern in the object.*

1. Highlight (select) drawn object(s).

2. Click **S**tyle .... `Alt` + `S`

3. Click **L**ines & Colors .... `L`

4. Choose one, or both, of the following:

   • Background color

   • Pattern color

5. Click **OK** .... `↵`

Group/Ungroup Drawn Object(s)

Enables you to move and style several drawn objects at the same time, if you group them together. When you want to work with the objects individually, ungroup them.

1. Highlight (select) objects you want to group.

   OR

   Highlight (select) group(s) you want to ungroup.

2. Click **E**dit .... `Alt` + `E`

3. Click **A**rrange .... `A`

4. Click **G**roup .... `G`

   OR

   Click **U**n**g**roup .... `G`

Flip Drawn Object(s)

Flips objects horizontally (backward) or vertically (upside down).

1. Highlight (select) drawn object(s).

2. Click **E**dit .... `Alt` + `E`

3. Click **A**rrange .... `A`

   To flip horizontally:

   Click **Flip L**eft-Right .... `L`

(continued...)

FLIP DRAWN OBJECT(S) (continued)

To flip vertically:

Click **Flip Top-Bottom** .... `T`

> NOTE: The following objects cannot be flipped: embedded objects, macro buttons, pictures, query tables and text blocks.

Rotate Drawn Object(s)

Rotates a drawn object on its axis.

1. Highlight (select) drawn object(s).

2. Click **Edit** .... `Alt` + `E`

3. Click **Arrange**.. `A`

4. Click **Rotate** .... `R`

5. Move mouse pointer the direction you want to rotate.

> NOTE: To rotate the drawn object in 45-degree segments, hold down Shift as you complete step 4.

6. Click mouse button when object is in desired position.

Shuffle Drawn Object(s)

Repositions an object in front (or back) of another object.

1. Highlight (select) drawn object(s).

2. Click **Edit** .... `Alt` + `E`

3. Click **Arrange**.. `A`

(continued...)

SHUFFLE DRAWN OBJECT(S) (continued)

4. Click **B**ring to Front .... `B`

   OR

   Click **S**end to Back .... `Esc`

Lock/Unlock Drawn Object(s)

Prevents anyone from changing a drawn object.

> *NOTE: When an object is locked, handles are*
> *shaped like diamonds.*

1. Highlight (select) drawn object(s).

2. Click **E**dit .... `Alt` + `E`

3. Click **A**rrange .... `A`

   To lock:

   Click L**o**ck .... `O`

   To unlock:

   Click Unl**o**ck .... `O`

Fasten Drawn Object(s)

By default, a drawn object is fastened to the cells behind
the top left and bottom right corners of the object. A
fastened object then changes position or size when cells
are deleted or inserted and other changes are made to the
worksheet. Use this procedure to change how an object
is fastened to the cells behind it.

(continued...)

FASTEN DRAWN OBJECT(S) (continued)

1. Highlight (select) drawn object(s).

2. Click **E**dit .... `Alt` + `E`

3. Click **A**rrange... `A`

4. Click **F**asten to cells.. `F`

   To move and size object, when you hide, move and size cells:

   Click **T**op left and bottom right cells .... `T`

   To move but not size object, when you hide, move and size cells:

   Click Top **l**eft cell only .... `L`

4. Click **OK** .... `↵`

EDIT ENTRY

(See UNDO (PREVIOUS COMMAND), page 146.)

While Typing

Press **Backspace** .... `Backspace`
to erase characters to left of cursor.

OR

Press **Esc** .... `Esc`
to cancel edit procedure.

OR

1. Press **F2** (Edit)... `F2`

(continued...)

EDIT ENTRY (continued)

2. Use cursor keys to correct entry.

3. Press **Enter** .... ⏎
   to place edited data into worksheet.

After Data Entry

-Classic keystrokes-

position cursor, F2, correct entry, ⏎

1. Double click cell to be edited.

2. Use arrow keys to correct entry .... ← →

3. Click **Confirm** button.

ELECTRONIC MAIL

Using a variety of electronic mail software packages, you can send a chart, drawn object, range or file as mail.

Send Mail (within 1-2-3)

1. Click **File** .... Alt + F

2. Click **Send Mail** .... M

3. Click **OK** .... ⏎

4. Use dialog box for sending mail as usual. When you are done, you will automatically return to 1-2-3.

58

Attach File (to Mail Message)

1. Create 1-2-3 file you want to attach.

2. Click **F**ile .... `Alt` + `F`

3. Click **Send M**ail .... `M`

4. Click **A**ttach .... `Alt` + `A`
   if file is not modified.

   OR

   Click **S**ave and attach .... `Alt` + `S`
   if file is modified or not saved.

5. Click **OK** .... `↵`

6. Use **File Save As** dialog box as usual, if you have never saved the file.

7. Use dialog box for sending mail as usual. When you are done, you will automatically return to 1-2-3.

Insert Chart, Object or Range (in Mail Message)

1. Highlight (select) chart, drawn object or range.

2. Click **File** .... `Alt` + `F`

3. Click **Send M**ail .... `M`

4. Click **OK** .... `↵`

5. Use dialog box for sending mail, as usual. When you are done, you will automatically return to 1-2-3.

EMBED OBJECT

While using 1-2-3, you can create information (text or graphics) in another Windows application and move the information into the current 1-2-3 file. This is called ***embedding an object.***

> *NOTE: When you embed an object, the information is stored in the .WK4 file.*

Embed New Object

1. Create file where the embedded object will appear.

2. Highlight (select) a cell near where you want object to appear.

> *NOTE: 1-2-3 will position the embedded object to the right of and below the selected cell.*

3. Click **E**dit .... `Alt` + `E`

4. Click **Insert Object** .... `O`

5. Highlight (select) type of object .... `↓` `↑` , `↵`
    you want to create.

6. Click **OK** .... `↵`

7. 1-2-3 opens application (or makes it active, if already open). Create desired text, object, etc.

8. Save your work in the other application.

9. Click **File Exit** or **File Exit & Return**, in the other application, to exit application and return to 1-2-3.

> *NOTE: Back in 1-2-3, you can double click the embedded object to restart the other application and edit the object.*

Embed Existing Object

1. From the other application, highlight object and copy or cut it to the clipboard.

2. Make the 1-2-3 file, in which you want to embed object, the current file.

3. Highlight (select) where you want object to appear.

   NOTE: 1-2-3 places the object slightly below and to the right of the range you highlight.

4. Click **Edit** .... `Alt` + `E`

5. Click **Paste Special** .... `S`

6. Highlight (select) format .... `↓` `↑` , `↵` of object.

7. Click **Paste** .... `Alt` + `P`

   NOTE: In 1-2-3, you can double click the embedded object to restart the other application and edit the object.

ENTER FORMULAS

Type Formula

1. Position cursor in cell to contain formula.

2. Type + ... `+`

3. Type desired formula using standard arithmetic symbols and cell names or locations. For example, +A3+B6 adds contents of A3 to contents of B6.

(continued...)

TYPE FORMULAS (continued)

> *NOTE:* *To type a formula with absolute values (that will not be changed, even if the contents of the cell changes), type a $ in front of the column letter and row number. For example, A3.*

4. Press **Enter** .... ⏎

Build Formula

1. Position cursor in cell to contain formula.

2. Type + ... +

3. Position cursor .... ↑ ↓ → ←
   in first cell of formula.

4. Type one of the following:

   + (addition) .... +

   - (subtraction) .... -

   * (multiplication) .... *

   / (division) .... /

5. Position cursor .... ↑ ↓ → ←
   in next cell of formula.

6. Repeat step 4.

7. Continue repeating steps 5 and 6 until last cell appears in formula.

8. Press **Enter** .... ⏎

Build Formula (with Absolute Values)

1. Complete steps 1-3, above.

2. Press **F4** (Absolute) .... `F4`

3. Repeat steps 4-5, above.

4. Repeat step 2 of this procedure.

5. Repeat steps 4-5, above.

6. Continue repeating steps 4 and 5 of this procedure until last cell appears in formula.

7. Press **Enter** .... `↵`

Update Formulas Linked to Other Files

-Classic keystrokes-

position cursor, `/` , `F` , `A` , `L`

1. Click **E**dit .... `Alt` + `E`

2. Click **L**inks .... `L`

   To change link types being updated:

   a. Click **L**ink type box .... `Alt` + `L`

   b. Click desired type .... `↓` `↑` , `↵`

3. Click Update **A**ll .... `A`

(continued...)

Type @Functions

(See FUNCTION DESCRIPTIONS, page 169.)

1. Position cursor in cell to contain function.

2. Click **@Function** button.

3. Click **List All** .... ↓ ↑ , ↵

   OR

   a. Click **Function** .... ↓ ↑ , ↵
      on menu.

   b. Skip to step 9.

4. Position cursor in **Category** .... Alt + C

5. Highlight desired category .... ↓ ↑ , ↵
   or **All**.

6. Position cursor in **Functions** .... Tab

7. Highlight desired function .... ↓ ↑ , ↵

8. Click **OK** .... ↵

9. Type your information for place holders.

10. Click **Confirm** button .... ↵

Customize @Function Menu

1. Click **@Function** button.

2. Click **List All**.

3. Click **Menu** .... Alt + E

(continued...)

CUSTOMIZE @FUNCTION MENU (continued)

To add @Function:

a. Position cursor....................... `Alt` + `F`
in **@Functions**.

b. Highlight function................ `↓` `↑` , `←`
to be added.

c. Click A**d**d .... `Alt` + `D`

To Remove @Function:

a. Position cursor....................... `Alt` + `M`
in **Current** **m**enu.

b. Highlight function................ `↓` `↑` , `←`
to be removed.

c. Click **R**emove .... `Alt` + `R`

To Separate menu @Functions:

a. Position cursor .... `Alt` + `M`
in **Current** **m**enu.

b. Highlight function................ `↓` `↑` , `←`
below which you
want separator.

c. Click Se**p**arator .... `Alt` + `P`

5. Click **OK**.. `←`

ENTER VALUES

Use the procedure below to type formulas, functions and numbers.

> *NOTE: To add note to value, type ; (semicolon) at end of value followed by note.*

1. Position cursor where you want to type a value.

2. Type value ....*value*

> *NOTE: If you enter a number with more than 15 decimals, 1-2-3 will round the number to 15 decimals.*

3. Click **Confirm** button ....   ,

ERASE

If necessary, save changes before erasing screen.

Screen/Worksheet

-Classic keystrokes-

1. Click **F**ile .... Alt + F

2. Click **C**lose.. C

3. Choose one of the following:

   • **Y**es.................................... Alt + Y

   • **N**o .... Alt + N

   • Cancel..................................... Esc

66

Cell or Range

*NOTE: Erased cells can be recovered. (See **UNDO (Previous Command)**, page 146.)*

-Classic keystrokes-

> position cursor, **/**, **R**, **E**

1. Highlight (select) cell(s) to be erased.

2. Press **Delete** .... Del

Cell Contents or Style

1. Highlight (select) cell(s) to be erased.

2. Click **Edit** .... Alt + E

3. Click **Clear** .... E

4. Choose one of the following:

   • Cell contents only .... Alt + C

   • Style only .... Alt + S

   • Both .... Alt + B

5. Click **OK** .... ↵

EXIT LOTUS 1-2-3

*(See **QUIT/EXIT**, page 120.)*

EXTERNAL DATABASE

Use the procedures on the next page to use 1-2-3 with an external database.

Connect to External Database

1. Click **T**ools .... `Alt` + `T`

2. Click **Data**b**ase** .... `B`

3. Click **C**onnect to External............................ `C`

4. Click driver .... `↓` `↑` , `↵`

5. Click **C**ontinue .... `Alt` + `C`

6. Click database table .... `↓` `↑` , `↵`

7. Click **C**ontinue .... `Alt` + `C`

8. Accept default range name.

   OR

   Type different range name ....*rangename*

9. Click **OK** .... `↵`

Create External Database

1. Click **T**ools .... `Alt` + `T`

2. Click **Data**b**ase** .... `B`

3. Click **Cr**eate **Table**.............................. `R`

4. Click driver .... `↓` `↑` , `↵`

(continued...)

EXTERNAL DATABASE (continued)

5. Click **C**ontinue .... `Alt` + `C`

6. Click database table .... `↓` `↑` , `↵`

7. Click **C**ontinue .... `Alt` + `C`

8. Accept default range name.

   OR

   Type different range name .... *rangename*

9. Click **C**ontinue .... `↵`

10. Type model table range .... *modeltablerange*

11. Type command, if required by driver .... *command*

12. Click **OK** .... `↵`

Send Command to External Database

1. Click **T**ools .... `Alt` + `T`

2. Click Data**b**ase .... `B`

3. Click **S**end Command .... `S`

4. Click driver .... `↓` `↑` , `↵`

5. Click **C**ontinue .... `↵`

   *NOTE: If driver you want does not display, use
   Install program to install driver.*

(continued...)

SEND COMMAND TO EXTERNAL DATABASE (continued)

6. Click **directory**.................... [↓] [↑] , [↵]
   or **external database table.**

7. Click **C**ontinue .... [↵]

8. Type command ....*command*

   *NOTE: You can enter up to 512 characters. Also,
   you can send more than one command at
   a time.*

9. Click **OK** .... [↵]

Disconnect from External Database

1. Click **T**ools .... [Alt] + [T]

2. Click **Data**b**ase** .... [B]

3. Click **Disc**o**nnect** .... [O]

4. Click name .... [↓] [↑] , [↵]
   from which you want
   to disconnect.

5. Click **OK** .... [↵]

FIND/REPLACE

*(See **SEARCH RANGE**, page 126.)*

FORMAT

There are three ways to change cell format in a worksheet: as a single cell, range or collection, as default settings for current worksheet and as default settings for current and future sessions.

Format Cell(s), Range or Collection

(See CHANGE APPEARANCE OF DATA, page 9.)

Worksheet Defaults

1. Click **Style** .... **Alt** + **S**

2. Click **Worksheet Defaults** .... **W**

3. Choose different Font, Size, Column width, Alignment and other settings, as desired.

4. Click **OK** .... **↵**

System Defaults

(See SET DEFAULTS USER SETUP, page 129.)

GRAPHS

(See CHART, page 18.)

GROUP MODE

This feature enables all worksheets in a file to take on worksheet settings of current worksheet. Changes made to any worksheet are mimicked in others.

Turn Group Mode On/Off

-Classic keystrokes-

| `/`, `W`, `G`, `G`, `E` or `D` |

1. Click **S**tyle .... `Alt` + `S`

2. Click **W**orksheet Defaults .... `W`

3. Click **G**roup mode .... `Alt` + `G`
   under **Other.**

4. Click **OK** .... `↵`

HELP

The Help menu offers several selections:

- **Contents**   Lists different types of Help topics.

- **Search**   Lets you type a word or two to find the Help topic you want.

- **Using Help**   Contains specific information about using Help.

- **Keyboard**   Contains specific information about using the keyboard in 1-2-3.

- **How Do I?**   Gives specific information on commonly used 1-2-3 tasks.

(continued...)

72

- *For Upgraders* *Describes 1-2-3 Classic commands.*

- *Tutorial* *Guides you though eight on-line lessons about 1-2-3.*

- *About 1-2-3* *Displays release number and copyright information.*

Use procedure below to display Help information using Search option.

1. Click **H**elp.. `Alt` + `H`

2. Click **S**earch .... `S`

3. Type name of topic..*topic*
   when **Search** dialog box appears.

4. Press **Enter**.. `↵`

5. Highlight desired topic................................. `↓` `↑`
   in the box at bottom.

6. Click **G**o To................................. `Alt` + `G` or `↵`
   after reading Help topic.

   To return to worksheet:

   a. Click **F**ile .... `Alt` + `F`

   b. Click E**x**it .... `X`

   To return to search screen:

   Click **S**earch .... `Alt` + `S`

Help for Current Procedure

Click **?** button in right corner.................................... `F1`

HIDE INFORMATION

Hide Column(s)

Hides selected columns without erasing data. Formulas in hidden columns continue to work correctly.

-Classic keystrokes-

/ , **W** , **C** , **H** , highlight column(s), **⏎**

1. Highlight (select) range .... **↑** **↓** **→** **←** , **⏎**

   NOTE: The range should include one cell in each column you want to hide.

2. Click **S**tyle .... **Alt** + **S**

3. Click **H**ide .... **H**

4. Click **C**olumn .... **Alt** + **C**

5. Click **OK** .... **⏎**

Redisplay Hidden Column(s)

-Classic keystrokes-

/ , **W** , **C** , **D**

1. Highlight (select) columns surrounding column(s) to redisplay.

2. Click **S**tyle .... **Alt** + **S**

3. Click **H**ide .... **H**

4. Click Sho**w** .... **Alt** + **W**

Hide Data in Range (or Collection)

1. Highlight range (or collection).

2. Click **S**tyle .... `Alt` + `S`

3. Click **N**umber Format .... `N`

4. Click **Hidden** .... `↓` `↑` , `↵`

5. Click **OK** .... `↵`

Redisplay Data in Range (or Collection)

1. Repeat steps 1-3, **Hide Data in Range (or Collection)**, above.

2. Click **R**eset .... `Alt` + `R`

Hide Worksheet(s)

1. Highlight (select) range .... `↑` `↓` `→` `←` , `↵`

   NOTE: The range should include one cell in each worksheet you want to hide.

2. Click **S**tyle .... `Alt` + `S`

3. Click **H**ide .... `H`

4. Click **S**heet .... `Alt` + `S`

5. Click **OK** .... `↵`

Redisplay Hidden Worksheet(s)

1. Highlight (select) worksheets surrounding worksheet(s) to redisplay:

   a. Double click letter at intersection of columns and rows (upper left corner) on worksheet before hidden worksheet(s).

   b. Move to worksheet after hidden worksheet(s).

   c. Double click letter at intersection of columns and rows (upper left corner).

2. Click **S**tyle .... Alt + S

3. Click **H**ide .... H

4. Click Sho**w** .... Alt + W

5. Click **OK** .... ↵

HIGHLIGHT (SELECT) RANGE

-Classic keystrokes-

position cursor, Shift + ↑ ↓ → ←, release Shift

1. Position mouse pointer in first cell to be highlighted (selected).

2. Press left mouse button.

3. Drag mouse pointer to last cell to be highlighted (selected).

4. Release left mouse button.

IF STATEMENT

*(See **Logical Functions**, page 70; **Enter Formulas**, page 60.)*

IMPORT FILE

-Classic keystrokes-

position cursor, **/** , **F** , **I** , **T** or **N** , file name, **↵**

1. Position cursor where imported data is to begin.

2. Click **File** .... **Alt** + **F**

3. Click **Open** .... **O**

4. Click **File type** .... **Alt** + **T**
   to see list of specific types of files.

5. a. Click **File name** .... **Alt** + **N**
      section of dialog box.

   b. Type name of file you want ....*filename*

   OR

   a. Click desired drive .... **↑** **↓** , **↵**
      under **Drives**.

   b. Click desired directory .... **↑** **↓** , **↵**
      under **Directories**.

   c. Click desired file name .... **↑** **↓** , **↵**
      under **File name**.

6. Click **OK** .... **↵**

INSERT/DELETE

Insert Columns/Rows

position cursor, **/**, **W**, **I**, **C** or **R**, highlight, **↵**

1. Highlight (select) as many columns or rows as you want to add to worksheet.

   NOTE: New columns will be placed to the left of the highlighted columns. New rows will be placed above the highlighted rows.

2. Click **E**dit...................................... **Alt** + **E**

3. Click **I**nsert .... **I**

4. Click **C**olumn .... **Alt** + **C**

   OR

   Click **R**ow .... **Alt** + **R**

5. Click **OK**.. **↵**

Delete Columns/Rows

position cursor, **/**, **W**, **D**, **C** or **R**, highlight, **↵**

1. Highlight (select) columns or rows you want to delete.

2. Click **E**dit...................................... **Alt** + **E**

3. Click **D**elete .... **D**

Insert Range

1. Highlight (select) range near where you want to insert same size range.

2. Click **E**dit .... `Alt` + `E`

3. Click **I**nsert .... `I`

4. Click **I**nsert selection .... `Alt` + `I`

5. Click **C**olumn .... `Alt` + `C`
   to shift range to right.

   OR

   Click **R**ow .... `Alt` + `R`
   to shift range down.

6. Click **OK** .... `←`

Delete Range

1. Highlight (select) range near what you want to delete.

2. Click **E**dit .... `Alt` + `E`

3. Click **D**elete .... `D`

4. Click **D**elete selection .... `Alt` + `D`

5. Click **C**olumn .... `Alt` + `C`
   if you want right range
   to shift left.

   OR

   Click **R**ow .... `Alt` + `R`
   if you want range below
   to shift up.

6. Click **OK** .... `←`

Insert Worksheet

You can have as many as 256 worksheets in a file.

1. Click **E**dit .... Alt + E

2. Click **I**nsert I

3. Click **S**heet .... Alt + S

4. Click **B**efore .... Alt + B

    OR

    Click **A**fter .... Alt + A

5. Click **Q**uantity .... Alt + Q

6. Type desired number ....*number*

    OR

    Click up or down arrow .... ↑ ↓
    to indicate number.

7. Click **OK** .... ↵

Delete Worksheet

1. Highlight (select) at least one cell in each worksheet
   you want to delete.

2. Click **E**dit .... Alt + E

3. Click **D**elete .... D

4. Click **S**heet .... Alt + S

5. Click **OK** .... ↵

JUSTIFY LABELS

Paragraphs can be created from columns of labels to fit into a specific width. NOTE: Continuous text will justify until a non-label entry is reached.

-Classic keystrokes-

`I`, `R`, `J`, highlight range, `↵`

1. Highlight (select) range to be justified.

2. Click **S**tyle .... `Alt` + `S`

3. Click **A**lignment .... `A`

4. Click desired setting(s). For example:

Under **Horizontal:**

- **L**eft .... `Alt` + `L`

- **C**enter .... `Alt` + `C`

- **R**ight .... `Alt` + `R`

Under **Vertical:**

- **T**op .... `Alt` + `T`

- Ce**n**ter .... `Alt` + `N`

- **B**ottom .... `Alt` + `B`

5. Click **OK** .... `↵`

LABELS

Text entries in 1-2-3 are called labels. A label can contain (and begin with) letters or numbers.

If the first character in a label is a letter, 1-2-3 automatically adds a label-prefix character.

If the first character in a label is a number, you must add a label-prefix character.

> *NOTE: Labels are left-aligned and numbers are right-aligned by default. To change these settings, use the Style Alignment command.*

Label-Prefix Characters

Character	Alignment
`'`	Left
`"`	Right
`^`	Center
`\`	Repeat

Enter Label

1. Place cursor in desired cell.

2. Type label text ....*label text*

> *NOTE: If label does not start with a letter, be sure to begin with one of the label-prefix characters shown above.*

3. Click **Confirm** button ....   or

LINES

*(See **CHANGE APPEARANCE OF DATA**, page 9.)*

LINKS

There are several ways to link information in 1-2-3. You choose a link method based on how much you want to control the process.

Link from Another Application (1-2-3's Choice)

1. Start application and open file.

2. Highlight (select) data to be included in 1-2-3 file.

3. Use **Edit Copy** command to copy selected data to Clipboard.

4. Return to 1-2-3 and open file where you want copied data.

5. Highlight (select) location where you want copied data to appear.

6. Click **Edit** .... `Alt` + `E`

7. Click **Paste Link** .... `K`

Link from Another Application (Your Choice)

1. Repeat steps 1-5, above.

2. Click **Edit** .... `Alt` + `E`

3. Click **Paste Special** .... `S`

4. Select a format in **Using Clipboard format** list box.

5. Click **Paste Link** .... `Alt` + `L`

Link 1-2-3 File to Another Application

1. Open 1-2-3 file.

2. Highlight (select) data, chart, drawn object, etc. to be included in 1-2-3 file.

3. Click **E**dit .... `Alt` + `E`

4. Click **C**opy .... `C`

5. Start the other application and open file you want to contain the link.

6. Indicate position where you want information in link to appear, if necessary.

7. Paste the link (e.g., Edit Paste Link, Edit Paste Special, depending on the application).

Get Information about DDE/OLE Links

1. Click **E**dit .... `Alt` + `E`

2. Click **L**inks .... `L`

3. Select link you want from list.

4. Click **Close** .... `⏎`

Edit Link

1. Click **E**dit .... `Alt` + `E`

2. Click **L**inks .... `L`

3. Select link you want to change from list.

4. Click **E**dit .... `Alt` + `E`

(continued...)

EDIT LINK (continued)

5. Change information in dialog box, as necessary.

   *NOTE: Under Update mode, select Automatic
   (updates link automatically when link is
   active) or Manual (updates link only when
   you choose Update in the Edit Links
   dialog box).*

6. Type range where you want to place linked data in
   Range text box.

7. Click **OK** .... ⏎

8. Click **Close** .... ⏎

Update/Delete/Deactivate Link

1. Click **Edit** .... Alt + E

2. Click **Links** L

3. Select link you want to change from list.

   To get new copy of data from server application:

   Click **Update All** .... Alt + A

   To delete link permanently:

   Click **Delete** .... Alt + D

   To stop updating link temporarily:

   Click **Deactivate** .... Alt + V

(continued...)

UPDATE/DELETE/DEACTIVATE LINK (continued...)

> *NOTE:* *When a link is deactivated, it is inactive and requires less memory. Changes in the source data will not appear in the 1-2-3 file until the link is updated. (To make the link active, click Update.)*

4. Click **Close**...

LIST FILES

Only Classic keystrokes are available for this feature.

Current Drive/Directory

-Classic keystrokes-

Different Drive/Directory

-Classic keystrokes-

Current Drive/Directory steps, **Esc**, **Esc**, new drive/directory,

filename, ↵

LOOKUP

*(See **Lookup Functions**, page 170.)*

MACROS

Store a macro to automate a 1-2-3 task. The basic procedure for creating a macro includes the following 8 steps:

1. Plan what the macro will do.

2. Choose where you want to enter the macro.

    NOTE: A macro can be stored in a regular worksheet file (with other data) or in a macro library (a file that contains only macros).

3. Enter macro commands.

4. Name the macro.

5. Run the macro.

6. Debug the macro.

    NOTE: This step is necessary only if the macro does not do what you want it to do in step 5.

7. Document the macro.

8. Save the macro.

Plan Macro

Planning macro commands and keystrokes saves time and helps you avoid mistakes.

Choose Where to Enter Macro

*If you are going to use a macro with only one worksheet, it makes sense to put the macro in that file. If, however, you are creating a macro to be used with several other worksheets, it makes more sense to put it in the **macro library**. The macro library is a worksheet file containing only macros.*

Enter Macro Commands

When entering macro commands, you record keystrokes, mouse actions, etc. in the Transcript window. Since some commands must be typed, it is important to use the correct syntax (structure).

Most macro commands begin with an open brace followed by the keyword (macro command name), a space, one or more arguments and a close brace. When typing macros:

- *Start and end a macro command in the same cell.*

- *The only blank space in a command should be the one between the keyword and the argument(s).*

Write Macro Command

1. Position cursor in the cell.

2. Type { (open brace) .... `{`

3. Press **F3** (NAME)... `F3`

4. Select keyword from list.................. `Tab` , `↓` `↑`

5. Click **OK** .... `↵`

6. Type any required and/or optional arguments.

7. Type } (close brace) .... `}`

8. Press **Enter**.. `↵`

Record Macro

To record macros, you must open the Transcript window. Then, perform the commands you want and 1-2-3 records them in the Transcript window. Finally, paste the recorded information into a worksheet to create a macro.

> NOTE: When you start 1-2-3, macro recording is off by default. After you turn it on, it stays on until you turn it off.

To clear Transcript window (if necessary):

a. Click **T**ools .... **Alt** + **T**

b. Click **M**acro .... **M**

c. Click **Show Tra**n**script** .... **N**

d. Click Transcript window.

e. Click **E**dit .... **Alt** + **E**

f. Click **Clea**r **All** .... **R**

1. Click **T**ools .... **Alt** + **T**

2. Click **M**acro .... **M**

3. Click Re**c**ord .... **C**

4. Enter command(s) and/or text you want to record.

Copy Recorded Macro

1. Click **T**ools .... **Alt** + **T**

2. Click **M**acro .... **M**

(continued...)

COPY RECORDED MACRO (continued)

3. Click **Show Transcript** .... N

4. Highlight (select) commands you want to copy.

5. Click **Edit** .... Alt + E

6. Click **Copy** C

   To paste macro into worksheet:

   a. Click a cell.

   b. Click **Edit** .... Alt + E

   c. Click **Paste** .... P

   To paste macro into button:

   a. Click **Tools** .... Alt + T

   b. Click **Macro** .... M

   c. Click **Assign to Button** .... Alt + A

   d. Click **Enter macro here** text box.

   e. Press **Shift+Insert** .... Shift + Ins

   *(See **Create Macro Button**, page 90.)*

   To paste macro into icon:

   a. Click **Tools** .... Alt + T

   b. Click **SmartIcons** I

(continued...)

COPY RECORDED MACRO (continued)

   c. Click **E**dit icon .... | E |

   d. Select the icon, to which you want to assign the macro, from the available icons.

   e. Click **Paste Macro** .... | Alt | + | M |

   f. Type description in **Description** text box, if desired.

   g. Click **OK** .... | ⏎ |

   h. Add new icon, if desired. *(See **SMARTICONS**, page 130.)*

Create Macro Button

1. Click **T**ools .... | Alt | + | T |

2. Click **D**raw .... | D |

3. Click **B**utton .... | B |

4. Place mouse pointer where you want button to appear.

   To create macro button in default size:

   Click.

   To create macro button in size you want:

   Drag across worksheet until button is desired size.

5. Type a descriptive name in the **Button text** text box to replace the default label "Button."

6. Click **OK** .... | ⏎ |

Assign Macro to Button

1. Press **Shift**+click (or use the lasso icon) to highlight button.

2. Click **T**ools .... `Alt` + `T`

3. Click **M**acro .... `M`

4. Click **A**ssign to Button .... `A`

5. Select **Range** in the Assign macro from drop-down box.

   OR

   Select **macro name** in the Existing named ranges list box.

   OR

   Specify **macro address** or **name** in the Range text box.

   NOTE: To see range names in another active file, double click file name and select desired macro name.

   To assign a macro from a button:

   Select **Button** in Assign macro from drop-down box.

   OR

   Enter **macro** in Enter macro here text box.

6. Type a descriptive name in the **Button text** text box to replace default label "Button."

7. Click **OK** .... `↵`

92

Name Macro

To name a macro, name the first cell using the Range Name command. You can name a macro using one of two methods: a backslash (\) followed by a single character, or a regular range name.

> *NOTE: To create an autoexecute macro, that runs every time the file is retrieved, name the macro 0 (zero).*

Run Macro

> *NOTE: To stop a macro while it is running, press Ctrl+BREAK. To clear the message that appears, click OK or press Esc.*

To run macro named with single character:

Hold down **Ctrl** and press the character.

To run multiple-character name:

Press **ALT+F3** (RUN)................. `Alt` + `F3`

OR

Press **Tools Macro Run** command.

To run macro you don't know the name of:

a. Highlight first cell of macro.

b. Complete the steps for a multiple-character name, above.

To run macro with button:

a. Make worksheet with button current.

(continued...)

RUN MACRO (continued)

> *NOTE:* If the button refers to a macro in a range,
> make sure the file containing the range is
> active.

b. Position cell pointer and click button.

To run macro from Transcript window:

a. Position cell pointer in worksheet using **Tools
Macro Show Transcript** command.

b. Highlight (select) macro commands you want
to run using **Transcript Playback** command.

Debug Macro

*1-2-3 offers two tools to help debug a macro. The **Step
mode** lets you run one macro command at a time. **Trace**
opens a window that displays the macro command about
to be performed. Then, if there's an error, Trace shows
the command causing the error.*

1. Position cell pointer in first cell of macro.

2. Click **T**ools .... Alt + T

3. Click **M**acro .... M

4. Click **S**ingle Step .... S

   OR

   Press **Alt+F2** (STEP) .... Alt + F2

5. Click **T**ools .... Alt + T

(continued...)

DEBUG MACRO (continued)

6. Click **M**acro .... M

7. Click **T**race... T

The Macro Trace window appears.

8. Run the macro.

9. Press any key to run the macro one command at a time.

10. Repeat steps 2-5, after fixing error, to turn off Step mode and close Macro Trace window.

Document Macro

After a macro runs correctly, it will be easier for you (and anyone else who wishes to use the macro) to access if you document it. To document the macro's name, enter a label in the cell to the immediate left of the macro's first cell.

Lotus also recommends that you describe the macro's function in the rows above the macro. And, if necessary, to document commands and subroutines, type a description in the cells to the right of the macro.

Save Macro

You can save a macro the same way you save any other data—using either the File Save As or File Save command.

MOVE

(See CUT/PASTE, page 38.)

MOVE CELL CURSOR

To Move:	Press:
Up/Down One Row	↑ ↓
Left/Right One Column	← →
One Screen Left	Ctrl + ← or Shift + Tab
One Screen Right	Ctrl + → or Tab
Up/Down Current Column	End + ↑ ↓
Left/Right Current Row	End + ← →
Bottom Right Corner of Active Area	End + Home
A1 (if not hidden and titles are not set)	Home
Up/Down One Screen	PgUp PgDn

Move to Specific Page/Menu

1. Click **E**dit .... Alt + E

2. Click **G**o To .... G

3. Type page number .... *number*

4. Click **OK** .... ↵

Move to Specific Page/Function Key

1. Press **F5** (GOTO) .... `F5`

2. Type page number ....*number*

3. Click **OK** .... `←┘`

NEW FILE

*Before you work in a file, it must be open. Use this procedure to open a new file. (See **OPEN FILE**, page 97, to open an existing file.)*

-Classic keystrokes-

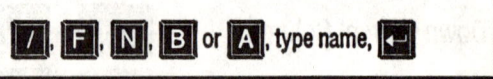

1. Click **F**ile .... `Alt` + `F`

2. Click **N**ew .... `N`

> NOTE: *1-2-3 automatically assigns a default name. The first time you save the file, 1-2-3 will replace the default name with the name you assign.*

NUMBERS

Number entries in 1-2-3 are called values.

> NOTE: *Numbers are right-aligned and labels are left-aligned by default. To change these settings, use the Style Alignment command.*

Enter Value

When typing a value in step 2 (below), the value must begin with a number from 0 to 9, or a decimal point. Also, be sure to start any negative number with a minus sign.

1. Place cursor in desired cell.

2. Type value ....*value*

> NOTE: If the value has more than 15 decimal places, 1-2-3 automatically rounds it to15 places. If you see asterisks (***) the entry is too long to fit in the column. (1-2-3 stores the value in the cell, but cannot display it.) To see the entry, double click the right border of the column.

3. Click **Confirm** button ....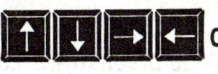

OPEN FILE

-Classic keystrokes-

1. Click **F**ile ....Alt + F

2. Click **O**pen ....O

(continued...)

OPEN FILE (continued)

3. Select type of file from **File Type** drop down list.

    To indicate file you want to open:

    Type file name ....*filename*
    in **File Name** text box.

    OR

    Select desired file in **Use File Name** and **Directories**
    list boxes and **Drives** drop down box.

4. Click **OK** .... ⏎

PAGE BREAK

Inserts page break in worksheet.

> *NOTE: If you use Classic keystrokes to insert a*
> *page break, the traditional "dot" symbol*
> *appears on the screen. If you use the*
> *other keystrokes, a dotted line appears to*
> *indicate a page break.*

-Classic keystrokes-

position cursor, **/**, **W**, **P**

---

1. Click cell one row below or one column to the
    right of where you want to place page break.

2. Click **S**tyle .... **Alt** + **S**

3. Click **Page B**reak .... **B**

(continued...)

PAGE BREAK (continued)

4. Click **R**ow...................................... Alt + R

   OR

   Click **C**olumn................................ Alt + C

5. Click **OK**.. ⏎

Remove Page Break

-Classic keystrokes-

> position cursor in cell w/ page break, **/** , **W** , **D** , **C** or
>
> **R** , ⏎

1. Click cell one row below or one column to the right of where you want to remove page break.

2. Click **S**tyle.................................... Alt + S

3. Click **Page B**reak.............................. B

4. Click **R**ow...................................... Alt + R
   to deselect.

   OR

   Click **C**olumn................................ Alt + C
   to deselect.

5. Click **OK**.. ⏎

PAGE SETUP

(See PRINT, pages 100.)

100

PASTE

*(See **COPY/PASTE**, page 36; **CUT/PASTE**, pages 38.)*

PREVIEW

*(See **Print Preview**, pages 107.)*

PRINT

Print Range/Collection

-Classic keystrokes-

position cursor, `/`, `P`, `P`, `R`, `.`, highlight
range/collection, `←`, `A`, `G`, `Q`

1. Highlight (select) range/collection.

2. Click <u>F</u>ile .... `Alt` + `F`

3. Click <u>P</u>rint .... `P`

4. Click OK .... `←`

Print File

-Classic keystrokes-

position cursor, `/`, `P`, `P`, `R`, `.`, highlight range,
`←`, `A`, `G`, `Q`

1. Position cursor in worksheet you want to print.

   OR

   Position cursor in any worksheet of file you want to print.

(continued...)

PRINT FILE (continued)

2. Click **F**ile .... `Alt` + `F`

3. Click **P**rint .... `P`

4. Click **Current w**orksheet .... `Alt` + `W`

   OR

   Click **A**ll worksheets .... `Alt` + `A`

5. Click **OK** .... `↵`

Print Drawn Objects Only

Use this procedure to print charts, lines, arrows, pictures and other drawn objects.

1. Highlight (select) drawn object(s).

2. Click **F**ile .... `Alt` + `F`

3. Click **P**rint .... `P`

4. Click **OK** .... `↵`

Print Range or File to ASCII File (on Disk)

Only Classic keystrokes are available for this procedure.

> *NOTE: A .PRN extension is automatically assigned to file.*

-Classic keystrokes-

position cursor, `/`, `P`, `F`, type name, `↵`, `R`,

highlight range, `↵`, `O`, `M`, `N`, `O`, `U`, `Esc`, `A`,

`G`, `Q`

102

Print Encoded File

Only Classic keystrokes are available for this procedure.

-Classic keystrokes-

position cursor, **[/]**, **[P]**, **[E]**, type name, **[↵]**, **[R]**, **[.]**,
highlight range, select options, **[↵]**, **[A]**, **[G]**, **[Q]**

Control Printer

To control printer in any Windows application, use Windows Print Manager.

-Classic keystrokes-

[/], **[P]**, **[S]** or **[R]** or **[C]**

Change Print Margins

1. Click **File** .... **[Alt]** + **[F]**

2. Click **Page Setup** .... **[G]**

3. Select margin option:

   - **Top** .... **[Alt]** + **[T]**

   - **Bottom** .... **[Alt]** + **[B]**

   - **Left** .... **[Alt]** + **[L]**

   - **Right** .... **[Alt]** + **[R]**

4. Type measurement .... *measurement*

   NOTE: To indicate margin in millimeters or centimeters, type mm or cm after measurement number.

5. Click **OK** .... **[↵]**

Add Print Titles

1. Click <u>F</u>ile .... `Alt` + `F`

2. Click **Pa<u>g</u>e Setup** .... `G`

3. Select title option:

   a. <u>C</u>olumns .... `Alt` + `C`

   b. Type range for vertical titles .... *range*

   OR

   a. Ro<u>w</u>s .... `Alt` + `R`

   b. Type range for horizontal titles .... *range*

4. Click **OK** .... `↵`

Add Headers/Footers

Headers are text printed below the top margin of each page in a file. Footers are printed above the bottom margin. Headers/Footers can be up to 512 characters long. 1-2-3 does not print any text beyond the right margin. When typing header and/or footer text, use the symbols shown below.

To enter:	Type:
Page number	#
Date (of printing)	@
Time (of printing)	+
File name	^
Contents of cell	\celladdress or cellname

-Classic keystrokes-

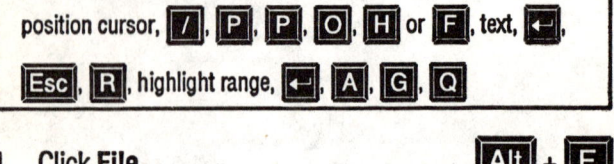

position cursor, **/**, **P**, **P**, **O**, **H** or **F**, text, **↵**, **Esc**, **R**, highlight range, **↵**, **A**, **G**, **Q**

1. Click **F**ile .... **Alt** + **F**

2. Click **Page Setup** .... **G**

The Page Setup dialog box appears. Three boxes appear next to Header and Footer. To left flush header/footer text, type in left box. To center text, type in center box. To right flush, type in right box.

3. Click **H**eader .... **Alt** + **H**

(continued...)

ADD HEADERS/FOOTERS (continued)

4. Press **Tab** .... `Tab`
   to position in different box,
   if necessary.

5. Type header text .... *text*

   AND/OR

   a. Click **F**ooter .... `Alt` + `F`

   b. Press **Tab** to position .... `Tab`
      in different box, if necessary.

   c. Type footer text .... *text*

6. Click **OK** .... `←`

Change Size of Printed Data

1. Click **File** .... `Alt` + `F`

2. Click **Pa**g**e Setup** .... `G`

3. Click **Si**z**e** .... `Alt` + `Z`

4. Click desired choice .... `↑` `↓` , `←`

   *NOTE: If you choose Manually scale option, type
   desired percentage in text box.*

5. Click **OK** .... `←`

Change Page Orientation

1. Click **File** .... Alt + F

2. Click **Pa̱ge Setup** .... G

3. Click **P̱ortrait** .... Alt + P

   OR

   Click **Lanḏscape** .... Alt + D

4. Click **OK** .... ⏎

Hide/Show Worksheet Elements

Use this procedure to determine whether or not frames, drawn objects and grid lines appear in the printed version of a worksheet.

1. Click **F̱ile** .... Alt + F

2. Click **Pa̱ge Setup** .... G

3. Choose one of the following to hide/show elements:

   • Woṟksheet frame .... Alt + K

   • Drawn o̱bject .... Alt + O

   • G̱rid lines .... Alt + G

4. Click **OK** .... ⏎

Named Page Settings

You can change setting under Page Setup and name specific combinations of the settings. Then, to quickly use the setting again, specify the name.

Name and Save Page Setting

1. Click **File** .... `Alt` + `F`

2. Click **Page Setup** .... `G`

3. Make desired changes in **Page Setup** dialog box. (See procedures, above.)

4. Click **Save** .... `Alt` + `S`

5. Type unique name (up to 15 characters).

6. Click **OK** twice .... `←` , `←`

> *NOTE: 1-2-3 saves named page settings with a .AL4 extension.*

Use Named Page Setting

1. Click **File** .... `Alt` + `F`

2. Click **Page Setup** .... `G`

3. Click **Retrieve** .... `Alt` + `V`

4. Click desired name .... `↑` `↓` , `←` , `Tab`

5. Click **OK** twice .... `←` `←`

Print Preview

To see how your pages will look when printed, use Print Preview. This feature is especially useful for checking placement of headers/footers, page breaks, etc.

1. Highlight (select) document you want to preview.

2. Click **File** .... `Alt` + `F`

(continued...)

PRINT PREVIEW (continued)

3. Click <u>P</u>rint.. `P`

4. Click **Print Pre<u>v</u>iew** .... `Alt` + `V`

5. Choose one of the following options:

   • Current <u>w</u>orksheet.................. `Alt` + `W`

   • <u>A</u>ll worksheets........................ `Alt` + `A`

   • Select <u>r</u>ange............................ `Alt` + `R`

6. Click **OK**.. `↵`

PROTECT WORKSHEET

There are three different ways to protect a worksheet:
password, ***seal*** *and* ***reservation***. *You can assign a*
password when you save the file. This feature stops
anyone who does not know the password from opening
the file. (See **Save With Password**, *page 124.)*

You can also seal a file with a password. This prevents
changes to contents, settings and styles. Others,
however, can open the file. If you want others to be able
to change some sections of the file, you can leave some
areas unprotected.

Finally, when you have the reservation to a file, you are
the only person who can save changes to it. This feature
is helpful when sharing files on a network.

Seal File

1. Display file you want sealed.

2. Click **File** .... `Alt` + `F`

3. Click **Protect** .... `R`

4. Click **Seal File** .... `Alt` + `S`

5. Click **OK** .... `↵`

6. Type password .... *password*

   NOTE: *This password is different than the password used when saving a file.*

7. Click **Verify** .... `Alt` + `V`

8. Type same password typed in step 6 .... *password*

9. Click **OK** .... `↵`

   NOTE: *The menu commands that cannot be used when a file is sealed are automatically dimmed.*

Seal File (with Unprotected Ranges)

1. Highlight (Select) range or collection where you want to allow changes.

2. Click **Style** .... `Alt` + `S`

3. Click **Protection** .... `P`

4. Click **Keep data unprotected** .... `Alt` + `K`
   after file is sealed.

5. Click **OK** .... `↵`

6. Complete **Seal File** procedure, above.

Reprotect Ranges

Use this procedure to protect ranges previously unprotected.

1. Click **File** .... `Alt` + `F`

2. Click **Protect** .... `R`

3. Click **Seal File** .... `Alt` + `S`

4. Click **OK** .... `←`

5. Highlight (select) unprotected range or collection you want to reprotect.

6. Click **Style** .... `Alt` + `S`

7. Click **Protection** .... `P`

8. Click **Keep data unprotected** .... `Alt` + `K`
   after file is sealed.

9. Click **OK** .... `←`

10. Complete **Seal File (with Unprotected Ranges)** above.

Get Reservation

Use this procedure to get the reservation for the current file, if it is available.

> *NOTE: When you have the reservation, you are the only one who can save changes to the file.*

1. Click **File** .... `Alt` + `F`

2. Click **Protect** .... `R`

3. Click **Get** .... `Alt` + `G`

Release Reservation

1. Click File .... `Alt` + `F`

2. Click Protect .... `R`

3. Click Release .... `Alt` + `R`

Turn Automatic Reservation On/Off

When this feature is turned on, the first user who reads the file into memory has the reservation.

1. Click File .... `Alt` + `F`

2. Click Protect .... `R`

3. Click Get reservation automatically .... `Alt` + `A`

4. Click OK .... `←`

QUICK COPY

(See COPY/PASTE, page 36.)

QUICK MENUS

*1-2-3 Release 4 for Windows contains a special feature called **Quick Menus**. You can use it to quickly access commonly used menu commands.*

To use a quick menu, highlight (select) chart, data or drawn object you want to change. Then, press right mouse button. 1-2-3 will display menu commands you might need, depending on what you highlighted.

For example, if you highlighted data, the quick menu will contain commands like Copy, Cut, etc. If you highlighted a chart or drawn object, though, other commands will be displayed.

QUERY DATABASE

Create Database Table

1. Type field names in adjacent cells in top row.

   NOTE: This is the first row of the table.

2. Enter information for first record below field names.

3. Enter information for each record in remaining rows.

   NOTE: Do not leave empty rows between records.

4. Assign a name to database with **Range Name**, if desired.

   NOTE: The row containing the field names must be the first row of the range. Also, do not use a name that matches a field name in this or any other table.

5. Add styles, if desired. (*See* **STYLES**, *page 141.*)

Create Query Table

A query table is a place on a worksheet where you can manipulate data from a database table.

NOTE: If you specify a multiple-cell range in step 10, only the fields and records that fit in the range will be displayed. In other words, 1-2-3 may find more records than are displayed if multiple-cell range is specified.

1. Click **T**ools .... `Alt` + `T`

2. Click **Data**b**ase** .... `B`

(continued...)

CREATE QUERY TABLE (continued)

3. Click **N**ew Query.. ⌨N

4. Type range containing database table.......... *tablerange*

5. Click **Choose Fields**................................. ⌨Alt + ⌨F

6. Indicate which fields will appear in query table by completing **Choose Fields**, below.

7. Click **Set Criteria** .... ⌨Alt + ⌨C

8. Indicate criteria used in query by completing **Set Criteria**, below.

9. Click **Select location for** .... ⌨Alt + ⌨Q
   new **q**uery table.

10. Type top left cell of range... *cell*

   NOTE: The query table will write over any existing data in the range.

   OR

   Type multiple cell range .... *cellrange*

11. Click **OK** .... ⌨↵

Choose Fields

To choose fields for new query table:

a. Highlight (select) range containing database table.

b. Click **Tools** .... `Alt` + `T`

c. Click **Database** .... `B`

d. Click **New Query** .... `N`

e. Click **Choose Fields** .... `Alt` + `F`

f. Click **OK** .... `←`

To choose fields for existing query table:

a. Highlight (select) query table.

b. Click **Query** .... `Alt` + `Q`

c. Click **Choose Fields** .... `C`

d. Click **OK** .... `←`

To add field:

a. Click **Add** .... `Alt` + `A`

b. Highlight field name .... `↓` `↑` , `←`

c. Select **Option** under **Insert**.

d. Click **OK** .... `←`

(continued...)

CHOOSE FIELDS (continued)

To delete fields:

a. Highlight field names............ ↓ ↑ , ↵

b. Click **C**lear.................... Alt + C

c. Click **OK**.......................... ↵

To change field order:

a. Highlight field .... ↓ ↑ , ↵

b. Click up or down .... ↓ ↑

c. Click **OK**.......................... ↵

Set Criteria

To set criteria for new query table:

a. Highlight (select) range containing database table.

b. Click **T**ools .... Alt + T

c. Click Data**b**ase .... B

d. Click **N**ew Query..................... Alt + N

e. Click Set **C**riteria.................... Alt + C

f. Click **OK**.......................... ↵

(continued...)

SET CRITERIA (continued)

To set criteria for existing query table:

a. Highlight (select) query table.

b. Click **Query** .... `Alt` + `Q`

c. Click **Set Criteria** .... `C`

d. Click **OK** .... `↵`

To specify criterion for field:

a. Select field .... `Alt` + `F`
   from **Field** drop-down box.

b. Select logical operator .... `Alt` + `E`
   from **Operator**
   drop-down box.

c. Select value .... `Alt` + `V`
   from **Value** drop-down box.

d. Click **OK** .... `↵`

To limit record number:

a. Click **And** .... `Alt` + `A`

b. Follow **To specify criterion for field,** above.

c. Click **OK** .... `↵`

(continued...)

SET CRITERIA (continued)

To expand number of records:

a. Click **O**r .... `Alt` + `O`

b. Follow **To specify criterion for field**, above.

c. Click **OK** .... `←`

To remove criterion:

a. Highlight criterion you wish to remove.

b. Click **C**lear .... `Alt` + `C`

c. Click **OK** .... `←`

To apply changed criteria:

a. Click **R**efresh .... `Alt` + `R`
   without closing dialog box.

b. Click **OK** .... `←`

To limit number of records found:

a. Click **L**imit records .... `Alt` + `L`

b. Type desired number of records .... *number*

c. Click **OK** .... `←`

Find Records

1. Highlight (select) database table range.

2. Click **Tools** .... `Alt` + `T`

3. Click **Database** .... `B`

4. Click **Find Records** .... `F`

   To specify field criterion:

   a. Select field .... `Alt` + `F`
      from **Field** drop-down box.

   b. Select logical operator .... `Alt` + `E`
      from **Operator**
      drop-down box.

   c. Select value .... `Alt` + `V`
      from **Value** drop-down box.

   d. Click **OK** .... `↵`

   To limit number of records:

   a. Click **And** .... `Alt` + `A`

   b. Follow **To specify field criterion**, above.

   c. Click **OK** .... `↵`

   To expand number of records:

   a. Click **Or** .... `Alt` + `O`

   b. Follow **To specify field criterion**, above.

   c. Click **OK** .... `↵`

(continued...)

FIND RECORDS (continued)

> *NOTE:* *The records that meet your criteria are highlighted.*

To:	Press:
Edit data in record	**F2** , *make edits,* **↵**
Deselect highlighted records	**Esc** or *click any cell*
Go to next record	**Ctrl** + **↵**
Go to previous record	**Ctrl** + **Shift** + **↵**
Go to next cell in record	**↵**
Go to previous cell in record	**Shift** + **↵**

Rename Query Table

1. Highlight (select) query table.

2. Click **Q**uery .... **Alt** + **Q**

3. Click **N**ame .... **N**

4. Type new name..*table name*

    > *NOTE:* *The name can be up to 15 characters long.*

5. Click **R**ename .... **Alt** + **R**

Refresh Query Table

1. Highlight (select) query table.

2. Click **Q**uery .... **Alt** + **Q**

3. Click **R**efresh Now... **R**

Update Database Table

Updates a database table to reflect changes in the query table.

1. Click **Query** .... `Alt` + `Q`

2. Click **Set Options** .... `O`

3. Click **Allow updates** .... `Alt` + `A`
   to database table.

4. Click **OK** .... `↵`

5. Edit query table, as desired.

6. Click **Query** .... `Alt` + `Q`

7. Click **Update Database Table** .... `U`

QUIT/EXIT

-Classic keystrokes-

`/`, `W`, `Y` or `N`

1. Click **File** .... `Alt` + `F`

2. Click **Exit** .... `X`

3. Choose one of the following:

   • **Yes** .... `Y`

   • **No** .... `N`

   • Cancel .... `Esc`

   • **Save all** .... `S`

REPEATING CHARACTERS

This procedure may be used for repeating any character within a cell.

1. Place cursor in cell where character is to begin repeating.

2. Press \ (Backslash).. [\ ]
   to activate repeat action.

3. Press - (Hyphen) or = (Equal) .... [-] or [=]
   or another desired character.

4. Press **Enter**.. [↵]

5. Use Copy procedure to copy a line to another cell or range of cells. *(See **COPY/PASTE**, page 36.)*

RETRIEVE (OPEN) FILE

Retrieved worksheet will replace the worksheet currently on screen.

-Classic keystrokes-

[I], [F], [R], type a highlight name, [↵]

1. Click **F**ile .... [Alt] + [F]

2. Click **O**pen .... [O]

3. Type or click file name.................... [Tab], [↑] [↓]
   to be retrieved.

4. Click **OK** .... [↵]

122

In Different Drive/Directory

1. Click **F**ile .... `Alt` + `F`

2. Click **O**pen .... `O`

3. Click **D**irectories .... `Alt` + `D`

   AND/OR

   Click **Dri̲ves** .... `Alt` + `V`

4. Highlight drive/directory .... `↑` `↓` `→` `←`

5. Type or click **File n̲ame** .... `Alt` + `N`, `↑` `↓`

6. Click **OK** .... `↵`

SAVE FILE

When a file is saved, Lotus 1-2-3 Release 4 for Windows assigns a .wk4 extension to the file name unless a different extension is specified.

New Worksheet

-Classic keystrokes-

`I`, `F`, `S`, type path and File name, `↵`

1. Click **F**ile .... `Alt` + `F`

2. Click **Save A̲s** .... `A`

(continued...)

NEW WORKSHEET (continued)

3. Type file name...*filename*
   to save into current directory.

   OR

   Choose one of the following to save into different
   directory:

   • Click Dri**v**ers .... [Alt] + [V]

   • Click **D**irectories .... [Alt] + [D]

   • Highlight drive/directory . [↑] [↓] [→] [←]

   • Type file name ....*filename*

4. Click **OK** .... [↵]

Resave/Overwrite

[I], [F], [S], [↵], [C] or [R] or [B]

1. Click **F**ile .... [Alt] + [F]

2. Click **S**ave .... [S]

Portion of Current Worksheet as New File

-Classic keystrokes-

1. Highlight range of worksheet to be saved as separate file.

2. Click **F**ile... Alt + F

3. Click **Save as**.. A

4. Click **File name** box............................... Alt + N

5. Type new file name...*filename*

6. Click **Selected range only** .... Alt + S

7. Click **OK** .... ↵

Save with Password

Password names can contain up to 15 characters and are case sensitive.

-Classic keystrokes-

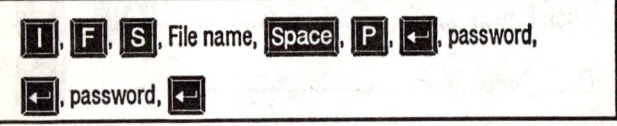

1. Click **F**ile.. Alt + F

2. Click **Save As**.. A

3. Click **File name** box............................... Alt + N

(continued...)

SAVE WITH PASSWORD (continued)

4. Type new file name...*filename*

5. Click **With password** .... `Alt` + `W`

6. Click **OK**.. `←`

7. Type password ....*password*

8. Click **Verify** box.................................... `Alt` + `V`

9. Type password ....*password*

10. Click **OK**.. `←`

Change Password

-Classic keystrokes-

`I` , `F` , `S` , `Backspace` , password, `←` , password, `←`

(See Save with Password, page 124.)

Delete Password

-Classic keystrokes-

`I` , `F` , `S` , `Backspace` , `←` , `R`

1. Follow steps 1-4, **Save with Password**, page 124.

2. Click **With password** .... `Alt` + `W`
    to clear X in box.

3. Click **OK**.. `←`

4. Click **Replace**.. `Alt` + `R`
    to update file without a password.

126

SEARCH RANGE

For Character Strings

Searches for character strings in labels and/or formulas within specified range.

-Classic keystrokes-

| [/], [R], [S], highlight range, [↵], type string, [↵], [F] |
| or [L] or [B], [F], [N] or [Q] |

1. Highlight (select) range to be searched.

2. Click **E̲dit** .... [Alt] + [E]

3. Click **F̲ind & Replace** .... [F]

4. Type string of characters .... *characterstring*
   for which you are searching.

5. Click **F̲ind** .... [Alt] + [F]

6. Click **All wor̲ksheets** .... [Alt] + [K]

   OR

   Click **Se̲lected range** .... [Alt] + [E]

7. Choose one of the following to indicate what you
   are searching for:

   • L̲abels .... [Alt] + [L]

   • F̲ormulas .... [Alt] + [O]

   • B̲oth (labels and formulas) .... [Alt] + [B]

(continued...)

FOR CHARACTER STRINGS (continued)

8. Click **OK** .... ⏎

9. Click **Find Next** .... Alt + N
   to find first instance.

10. Click **Find Next** .... Alt + N
    to find next instance.

    OR

    Click **Close** to stop search.

Replace Character String

Searches for character strings in labels and/or formulas within a specified range.

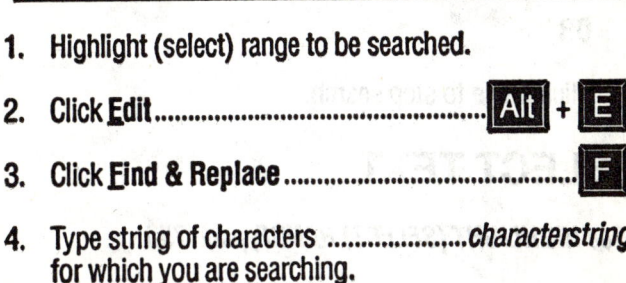

-Classic keystrokes-

1. Highlight (select) range to be searched.

2. Click **Edit** .... Alt + E

3. Click **Find & Replace** .... F

4. Type string of characters .... *characterstring*
   for which you are searching.

5. Click **Replace with** .... Alt + W

(continued...)

REPLACE CHARACTER STRING (continued)

6. Click **All worksheets**.............................. `Alt` + `K`

   OR

   Click **Selected range**.................... `Alt` + `E`

7. Click one of the following to indicate what you are searching for:

   • **Labels** .... `Alt` + `L`

   • **Formulas** .... `Alt` + `O`

   • **Both** (labels and formulas)....... `Alt` + `B`

8. Click **OK** .... `↵`

9. Click **Find Next** .... `Alt` + `N`
   to find first instance.

10. Click **Find Next** .... `Alt` + `N`
    to find next instance.

    OR

    Click **Close** to stop search.

SELECT TEXT

(See HIGHLIGHT (SELECT) RANGE, page 75.)

SET DEFAULTS (USER SETUP)

Use this procedure to change settings globally during the current work session. The current status of settings should be reviewed, before changes are made.

1. Click **Tools** .... `Alt` + `T`

2. Click **User Setup** .... `U`

3. Click one of the following to turn settings on/off under **Options:**

   - **D**rag-and-drop cells .... `Alt` + `D`

   - Use **A**utomatic format .... `Alt` + `A`

   - **S**ave files every .... `Alt` + `S`

   - **U**ndo .... `Alt` + `U`

   - Run autoexecute **m**acros .... `Alt` + `M`

   - **B**eep on error .... `Alt` + `B`

   - Number of recent **f**iles to show `Alt` + `F`

   NOTE: *If you choose Save files every or Number of recent files to show, you may also change the number for this option.*

   To change International settings (e.g., Format, Currency, etc.):

   a. Click **I**nternational .... `Alt` + `I`

   b. Make desired changes.

   c. Click **OK** .... `⏎`

(continued...)

130

To change Recalculation settings:

a. Click **R**ecalculation.................. `Alt` + `R`

b. Make desired changes.

c. Click **OK**.. `←`

To change name:

a. Click **N**ame................................ `Alt` + `N`

b. Type name..*name*

To change directory:

a. Click **W**orksheet directory........ `Alt` + `W`

b. Type path name ....*pathname*

4. Click **OK**..`←`

SMARTICONS

SmartIcons are special buttons that offer shortcuts for many commands and features. 1-2-3 comes with many different sets of SmartIcons.

For example, one set is displayed when you select a range. A different set is displayed when you select a chart. You can choose whether or not SmartIcons are displayed on screen. Also, you can choose where and how large they appear. For these and other procedures, see below.

Determine SmartIcon Purpose

1. Point to icon with mouse.

2. Hold down right mouse button.

Use SmartIcon

> *NOTE: You cannot use a SmartIcon with the keyboard.*

1. Select range, if necessary.

2. Click icon.

Select SmartIcon Set

1. Click **T**ools .... `Alt` + `T`

2. Click **SmartIcons** .... `I`

3. Click drop-down list .... `↵`
   of SmartIcon sets.

4. Click desired set .... `↓` `↑` , `↵`

5. Click **OK** .... `↵`

Show/Hide SmartIcon Set

1. Click **V**iew .... `Alt` + `V`

2. Click **Set View Preferences** .... `P`

3. Click **SmartIcons** .... `Alt` + `I`
   to select/deselect.

4. Click **OK** .... `↵`

Position SmartIcon Set

1. Click **T**ools .... `Alt` + `T`

2. Click **Smart**Icons .... `I`

3. Click **P**osition .... `Alt` + `P`

4. Click desired position .... `↓` `↑` , `↵`

5. Click **OK** .... `↵`

Position Icon in Set

1. Point to icon to be moved.

2. Hold down **Ctrl** and drag icon to desired location.

   *NOTE: To move icon to end of set, drag icon
   outside set.*

3. Release mouse button.

Size SmartIcons

1. Click **T**ools .... `Alt` + `T`

2. Click **Smart**Icons .... `I`

3. Click **M**edium .... `Alt` + `M`

   OR

   Click **L**arge .... `Alt` + `L`

4. Click **OK** .... `↵`

Delete SmartIcon Set(s)

1. Click **T**ools .... `Alt` + `T`

2. Click **SmartIcons** .... `I`

3. Click **D**elete Set .... `Alt` + `D`

4. Click set(s) to be deleted .... `↓` `↑` , `↵`

5. Click **OK** twice .... `↵` , `↵`

SOLVER

Use Solver to analyze and/or solve mathematical problems. You might use Solver when a worksheet includes:

- *Numbers*

- *Formulas*

- *Problems that can have more than one answer*

- *Several variables that must stay within certain limits*

To use Solver, you need to know the definition of four important terms:

Constraints   Formulas in the worksheet that indicate conditions each answer must satisfy.

Adjustable cells   Values Solver can change while attempting to satisfy restrictions described in the constraints.

(continued...)

134

Optimal cell   A cell containing a formula you want Solver to maximize (or minimize) with the constrains.

Optimal answer   The answer that maximizes (minimizes) the optimal cell.

*There are seven different types of **Solver reports**:*

Answer table   Lists all answers Solver found.

Cells used   Shows cells Solver used to find answers.

Differences   Compares two answers Solver found.

How solved   Summarizes how Solver found current answer.

Inconsistent constraints   Displays constraint cells that are not being satisfied by the current answer and shows how to adjust formulas to find an answer.

Nonbinding constraints   Displays constraint cells that are satisfied by the current answer but did not have an impact on the adjustable cell.

(continued...)

SOLVER (continued)

What-if limits   *Displays highest and lowest values you will find for each adjustable cell.*

Use this procedure to use Solver and, if desired, create an Answer table report.

1. Type problem in worksheet.

   NOTE: *Be sure you know the location of the Adjustable and Constraint cell(s).*

2. Click **R**ange... `Alt` + `R`

3. Click **A**nalyze.. `A`

4. Click **S**olver .... `S`

5. Click **A**djustable cells box...................... `Alt` + `A`

6. Type adjustable cell(s) ....*adjustablecell(s)*

7. Click **C**onstraint cells box .... `Alt` + `C`

8. Type constraint cell(s)........................*constraintcell(s)*

9. Click No. of ans**w**ers box .... `Alt` + `W`

10. Type number of answers ....*number* you want Solver to find (2 or more).

11. Click **S**olve... `Alt` + `S`

    NOTE: *When Solver finds an answer, it puts the answer in the worksheet and Solver Answer dialog box appears.*

(continued...)

SOLVER (continued)

12. Choose one of the following:

- **Next** .... `Alt` + `N`
  to see next answer.

- **Report** .... `Alt` + `R`
  to create report.

- **Close** .... `Esc`
  to close dialog box.

To create report of answers found:

a. Click **Answer** table .... `Alt` + `E`

b. Click **Table** .... `Alt` + `T`

*NOTE: Solver creates a new file. This file
contains information about the answers
Solver found.*

13. Click **Close** .... `Esc`

SORT DATA

By default, 1-2-3 sorts in the following order:

- *Blank cells*

- *Labels beginning with a blank space*

- *Labels beginning with numbers*

- *Labels beginning with letters (lowercase letters
  before uppercase letters)*

- *Labels beginning with other characters*

(continued...)

SORT DATA (continued)

The field you sort by is a sort key. You can have up to 255 sort keys.

-Classic keystrokes-

[/], [D], [S], [D], highlight range, [←], [P], position cursor, [←], [A] or [D], [←], [G]

1. Highlight (select) range to be sorted.

2. Click **R**ange...[Alt] + [R]

3. Click **S**ort ....[S]

4. Click field ....[←]
   you want to sort by
   in **Sort by** drop-down box.

   OR

   Select cell in field........[↑][↓][→][←], [←]

5. Click **A**scending ....[Alt] + [A]

   OR

   Click **D**escending ....[Alt] + [D]

6. Click **OK**...[←]

138

Sort on Additional Fields

-Classic keystrokes-

/, **D**, **S**, **D**, highlight range, **⏎**, **P**, position cursor,	
⏎, **A** or **D**, **⏎**, **E**, type number, **⏎**, position cursor,	
⏎, **A** or **D**, **⏎**, **G**	

1. Complete steps 1-5, above.

2. Click **Add Key**.......................................**Alt** + **K**

3. Repeat steps 4-5, above.

4. For each additional sort key, repeat steps 2 and 3 of this procedure.

5. Click **OK** ....**⏎**

SPELLER

Use the Spell Check feature to correct misspelled words and find duplicate words.

1. Click **Tools** ....**Alt** + **T**

2. Click **Spell Check**................................**C**

3. Choose one of the following under **Check:**

   - **Entire file** ....**Alt** + **E**
     to check current file or chart.

   - **Current worksheet**...............**Alt** + **C**
     to check current worksheet.

   - **Range**....................................**Alt** + **R**
     to check highlighted range.

(continued...)

SPELLER (continued)

4. Click **OK** .... ⏎

5. Choose one of the following when 1-2-3 finds an error or duplicate word:

    Click alternative word .... ↓ ↑ , ⏎

    OR

    a. Type new word to enter ....*word*

    b. Click **Replace** .... Alt + P
        to replace word
        in current instance.

    OR

    Click **Replace All** .... Alt + R
    to replace word
    in all instances.

    OR

    Click **Skip** or
    Skip All .... Alt + K or Alt + S
    to keep word
    unchanged.

    OR

    Click **Add To Dictionary** .... Alt + A
    to add word to dictionary.

    OR

    Press **Del** .... Del
    to delete duplicate word.

6. Click **Close** .... Alt + C
    to stop checking and save corrections.

STATUS BAR

The status bar appears on the bottom of the 1-2-3 screen. It displays information and lets you perform many procedures by using the mouse.

Automatic		Arial MT	12	08/30/93 10:49 AM				Menu

Number format indicator
Displays current number format. Click to change.

Decimal places indicator
Displays current number of decimal places. Click to change.

Named style indicator
Displays current named style. Click to change.

Typeface indicator
Displays current typeface. Click to change.

Point size indicator
Displays current point size. Click to change.

Date and time/ Row height and column width
Click to move between date and time and row height and column width displays.

E-Mail indicator
Click to read electronic mail if envelope appears.

SmartIcon button
Click to hide/show SmartIcons. Also, use to select a different set of SmartIcons.

Status indicator
Displays current status.

(continued...)

STATUS BAR (continued)

Circular reference Indicator *Click to go to circular reference if Circ displays.*

Calc indicator *Click to recalculate worksheet if Calc displays.*

Mode indicator *Displays current mode.*

STYLES

The alignment, borders, color, font and attributes, frames, number format and patterns of a cell make up its style. You can assign names for up to 16 different styles. Then, after you name a style, you can easily apply it to a range or collection.

*Besides creating 16 named styles, 1-2-3 offers 10 built-in styles. (See **Use Style Gallery**, page 143, for more information.)*

Name Style

1. Highlight (select) style you wish to name.

2. Click **Style**...**Alt** + **S**

3. Click **Named Style**...**S**

4. Position cursor ....**Alt** + **N**
   in **New style name** text box.

5. Type name (up to 15 characters)..................*stylename*

6. Click **OK**..**↵**

Apply Style

1. Highlight (select) range or collection.

2. Click style selector in status bar.

3. Click style from displayed list.

Delete Named Style

1. Click **S**tyle .... `Alt` + `S`

2. Click **Named S**tyle .... `S`

3. Highlight (select) style .... `↓` `↑`
   to be deleted.

4. Click **C**lear .... `Alt` + `C`

5. Click **Close**.

Copy Style

Use this feature to copy the style of a range or collection (alignment, font, etc.) from one range to another.

1. Highlight (select) range or collection whose style
   you want to copy.

2. Click **E**dit .... `Alt` + `E`

3. Click **C**opy .... `C`

4. Highlight (select) range or collection into which
   you want to paste styles.

5. Click **E**dit .... `Alt` + `E`

6. Click **Paste S**pecial .... `S`

(continued...)

COPY STYLE (continued)

7. Click **Styles only** .... $\boxed{Alt}$ + $\boxed{S}$
   under **Paste.**

8. Click **OK** .... $\boxed{\hookleftarrow}$

Delete Style

1. Highlight (select) range or collection whose style
   you want to copy.

2. Click **Edit** .... $\boxed{Alt}$ + $\boxed{E}$

3. Click **Clear** .... $\boxed{E}$

4. Click **Styles only** .... $\boxed{Alt}$ + $\boxed{S}$

5. Click **OK** .... $\boxed{\hookleftarrow}$

Use Style Gallery

1. Highlight range or collection you want to change.

2. Click **Style** .... $\boxed{Alt}$ + $\boxed{S}$

3. Click **Gallery** .... $\boxed{G}$

4. Click desired style name. (Notice displayed sample
   of chosen style.)

5. Click **OK** .... $\boxed{\hookleftarrow}$

TABS

Use tabs to name worksheets and move between worksheets in a file. Before you name worksheets in a file, they are named A, B, etc. After you name the worksheet, the name appears on the tab, where the letter was located.

Name Worksheet

When naming a worksheet, keep these guidelines in mind:

- *Names can be up to 15 characters long.*

- *You can use upper and lowercase letters, as well as a combination of the two, to name a worksheet.*

- *Do not use spaces in a worksheet name (use_instead).*

- *Do not start a name with ! (exclamation point).*

- *Do not include the following characters: ,(comma), .(period), ;(semicolon) or +, -, *, /, &, <, >, @, #, { or }.*

- *Do not use function or key names as worksheet names.*

- *Do not use names that look like cell addresses (e.g., FQ3).*

- *Do not use names that look like worksheet names (e.g., AA).*

1. Double click tab (at top of worksheet).

2. Type name ....*worksheetname*

3. Press Enter .... ⏎

Move Between Worksheets

To move to desired worksheet, click on the tab of the worksheet to which you want to move.

Delete Worksheet Name

1. Double click tab (at top of worksheet).

2. Press **Backspace** .... `Backspace` or `Del`
   or **Delete**.

3. Press **Enter** .... `←`

Hide/Show Worksheet Tabs

1. Click **View** .... `Alt` + `V`

2. Click **Set View Preferences** .... `P`

3. Click **Worksheet tabs** .... `Alt` + `T`
   to select/deselect option.

4. Click **OK** .... `←`

TRANSPOSE DATA

Transposes data from horizontal to vertical arrangement and vice versa. Formulas are replaced by values.

-Classic keystrokes-

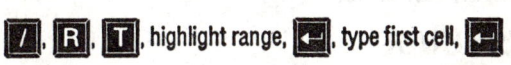
`/`, `R`, `T`, highlight range, `←`, type first cell, `←`

1. Highlight (select) range to be transposed.

2. Click **Range** .... `Alt` + `R`

(continued...)

146

TRANSPOSE DATA (continued)

3. Click **T**ranspose... `T`

4. Type first cell...*cell*
   to receive transposed data.

5. Click **OK** .... `⏎`

UNDO (PREVIOUS COMMAND)

Use the Undo feature to undo most commands. You cannot, however, undo the following:

* *Previous undo*

* *Cell pointer movement*

* *Changes to inactive worksheets*

* *Changes to files stored on disk*

* *Changes to the contents of the Clipboard*

* *Formula recalculation caused by F9 (CALC) or Edit Links command*

You must have Edit Undo enabled under User Setup before you can undo.

Enable UNDO

1. Click **T**ools .... `Alt` + `T`

2. Click **U**ser Setup................................. `U`

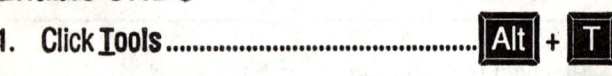

(continued...)

TO ENABLE UNDO (continued)

3. Click **U**ndo .... `Alt` + `U`

4. Click **OK** .... `↵`

UNDO

-Classic keystrokes-

`Ctrl` + `Z`

1. Click **E**dit .... `Alt` + `E`

2. Click **U**ndo .... `U`

VERSION MANAGER

*Use this feature to perform advanced what-if analysis. You can analyze your own data or data entered by other members of your workgroup. Version Manager has two ways of looking at data: **versions** and **scenarios**.*

Versions are sets of data for the same range. Each version has:

- *A date and time stamp*

- *A name*

- *An optional comment*

- *Optional styles*

The Version Manager is used to create and manage versions. Scenarios are named groups of versions.

(continued...)

148

VERSION MANAGER (continued)

*The Version Manager is divided into two sections: **Manager** and **Index**. Use Manager to work with one version at a time. Use Index to work with more than one version or scenario at a time.*

Create Version

1. Enter data for version into range.

2. Position cell pointer in range, if named.

   OR

   Select entire range, if unnamed.

3. Click **R**ange .... `Alt` + `R`

4. Click **V**ersion .... `V`

5. Click **C**reate .... `Alt` + `C`

6. Accept default range name.

   OR

   a. Click **R**ange name .... `Alt` + `R`

   b. Type range name ....*rangename* in text box.

(continued...)

CREATE VERSION (continued)

7. Accept default version name.

   OR

   a. Click **Version name**....................`Alt` + `V`

   b. Type version name.....................*versionname*
      in text box.

8. Save styles applied to version ....`Alt` + `T`
   by selecting **Retain styles**
   (selected by default).

9. Select Sharing option:

   • Unprotected.............................`Alt` + `U`

   • Protected ....`Alt` + `P`
     (selected by default).

   • Protected & hidden ....`Alt` + `H`

10. Click **OK** ....`↵`

Move Between Manager and Index

1. Click **Range**.................................`Alt` + `R`

2. Click **Version** ....`V`

3. Click **To Index** in *Manager* ....`Alt` + `T`

   OR

   Click **To Manager** in *Index* ....`Alt` + `T`

Move Between Version Manager and Worksheet

Click desired window.

OR

Press **Alt + F6**.................................... `Alt` + `F6`

Delete Versions

1. Click <u>R</u>ange.................................... `Alt` + `R`

2. Click <u>V</u>ersion .... `V`

3. Select version from **With version(s)** drop-down box in *Manager*.

   OR

   Select one or more versions in *Index*.

4. Click <u>D</u>elete .... `Alt` + `D`

5. Click **OK** .... `↵`

Display Version in Worksheet

1. Click <u>R</u>ange.................................... `Alt` + `R`

2. Click <u>V</u>ersion .... `V`

3. Click desired range in **Named <u>r</u>ange** drop-down box in *Manager*.

   OR

   Double click desired version in *Index*.

(continued...)

DISPLAY VERSION IN WORKSHEET (continued)

4. Click desired version in **With version(s)** drop-down box in *Manager*.

5. Click C**l**ose .... Alt + L

Display More than One Version

1. Click **R**ange.. Alt + R

2. Click **V**ersion V

3. Hold down **Ctrl** and click versions to be displayed in worksheet under *Index*.

4. Click Sho**w** .... Alt + W

Modify Version Settings

1. Click **R**ange.. Alt + R

2. Click **V**ersion V

3. Select version from **With versions** drop-down box in *Manager*.

   OR

   Select version from list in *Index*.

   NOTE: If the version you want to modify is hidden, use the Index. Choose Hidden only from the Shown box. Then, select the version you want to modify.

4. Click **I**nfo from *Manager* .... Alt + I

5. Follow step 9, **Create Version**, page 148.

6. Click **OK** .... ⏎

Update Versions

1. Click **R**ange.................................... `Alt` + `R`

2. Click **V**ersion .... `V`

3. Select the version from **With versions** drop-down box in *Manager*.

4. Enter new data and styles..............*newdata* and *styles* in worksheet.

5. Click **U**pdate in *Manager* .... `Alt` + `U`

6. Click **OK**.. `↵`

Create Version Report

1. Click **R**ange.................................... `Alt` + `R`

2. Click **V**ersion .... `V`

3. Click Re**p**ort in *Index*............................ `Alt` + `P`

4. Select range .... `Alt` + `R`
   in **R**eport on named
   range drop-down box.

5. Select version in **V**ersions list box.

6. Click **Version data** check box................. `Alt` + `D`
   to include data for selected versions.

7. Click **Audit information** check box........... `Alt` + `I`
   to include names of users who
   created versions and last modified
   version, with data and time
   version was created or last modified.

(continued...)

CREATE VERSION REPORT (continued)

8. Type address or name ....*celladdress* or *range*
   of range with formulas
   celladdress or range in
   Show results for this formula
   text box to see how versions
   change formula results.

9. Click **By columns** .... `Alt` + `C`

   OR

   Click **By rows** .... `Alt` + `W`

10. Click **OK** .... `↵`

Sort Versions

1. Click **Range** .... `Alt` + `R`

2. Click **Version** .... `V`

3. Click **Sort** drop-down box .... `Alt` + `O`
   in *Index*.

4. Choose sorting option .... `↑` `↓`

5. Click **OK** .... `↵`

Create Scenario

1. Click **Range** .... `Alt` + `R`

2. Click **Version** .... `V`

(continued...)

CREATE SCENARIO (continued)

3. Hold down **Ctrl** in *Index* .... `Ctrl`

4. Click versions to be grouped into scenario.

5. Click **S**cenario .... `Alt` + `S`

6. Accept default scenario name.

   OR

   a. Click **S**cenario name .... `Alt` + `S`

   b. Type scenario name .... *scenarioname*
      in text box

   To add comment:

   a. Click **C**omment text box .... `Alt` + `C`

   b. Type comment.

7. Select a Sharing option:

   • **U**nprotected .... `Alt` + `U`

   • **P**rotected .... `Alt` + `P`

   • Protected & **h**idden .... `Alt` + `H`

(continued...)

CREATE SCENARIO (continued)

To add version to scenario:

a. Select version in **Selected versions** list box.

b. Click << button.

OR

Double click version.

To remove version from scenario:

a. Select version in **Available versions** list box.

b. Click >> button.

OR

Double click version.

8. Click **OK** .... `↵`

Display Scenario

1. Click **Range** .... `Alt` + `R`

2. Click **Version** .... `V`

3. Select scenario in *Index.*

   NOTE: To display one scenario, double click it.

4. Click **Show** .... `Alt` + `W`

Modify Scenario

1. Click **R**ange.. `Alt` + `R`

2. Click **V**ersion .... `V`

3. Click **So**rt drop-down box......................... `Alt` + `O`
   in *Index*.

4. Click scenario.

   *NOTE: If scenario is hidden, click Hidden only
   option.*

5. Click **I**nfo... `Alt` + `I`

   To modify comment:

   a. Click **C**omment text box........... `Alt` + `C`

   b. Edit comment.

   To modify sharing option:

   Choose one of the following:

   - **U**nprotected................................ `Alt` + `U`

   - **P**rotected .... `Alt` + `P`

   - Protected & **h**idden .... `Alt` + `H`

   To add version to scenario:

   a. Select version in **A**vailable versions list box.

   b. Click << button.

   OR

   Double click version.

(continued...)

MODIFY SCENARIO (continued)

To remove version from scenario:

a. Select version in **Selected versions** list box.

b. Click >> button.

OR

Double click version.

6. Click **OK** .... ⏎

Delete Scenario(s)

1. Click **Range** .... Alt + R

2. Click **Version** V

3. Select scenario name(s) in **Sort** drop-down box under *Index*.

   OR

   Select one or more versions in *Index*.

4. Click **Delete** .... Alt + D

5. Click **OK** .... ⏎

WHAT-IF TABLES

A what-if table solves a question such as "How many more customer service employees do we need if our sales increase by 10%?" What-if tables are also helpful in analyzing different payment options for loans. For example, "What is the difference in monthly payments between a $100,000 loan for 10 years at 10.5% and a $100,000 loan for 15 years at 12%?"

What-if tables let you change one or more values in a formula. With 1-2-3 you can build three different types of tables:

•	***1-Variable What-If Table***	*Displays results of changing a single variable (in one or more formulas).*
•	***2-Variable What-If Table***	*Displays results of changing two values in a formula.*
•	***3-Variable What-If Table***	*Displays results of changing three values in a formula.*

Input Cell/Input Values

All what-if tables use two important items in calculations: input cell(s) and range(s) of input values.

•	***Input Cell(s)***	*Where 1-2-3 temporarily stores values for variable(s) during calculation.*

(continued...)

INPUT CELL/INPUT VALUES (continued)

NOTE: This cell is located outside of the table.

● **Range(s) of Input Values**   *Various numbers you want 1-2-3 to substitute in the formula during calculations.*

Create 1-Variable Table

1. Decide where to put the table in your worksheet. Be sure you have enough room for the formula, input values and results.

2. Position the input cell outside the table. If desired, enter a sample variable in the input cell.

3. Enter formula in second column of the first row of table.

4. Position each additional formula in adjacent column to the right (all in the same row) to use more than one formula.

   NOTE: Make sure the formula refers to the input cell.

5. Enter input values you want 1-2-3 to use in the first column of table, beginning in the second row.

   NOTE: Be sure to leave top left cell of the table blank.

Create 2-Variable Table

1. Decide where to put the table in your worksheet. Be sure you have enough room for the formula, two sets of input values and results.

2. Position the two input cells outside table. Enter a sample variable in each input cell, if desired.

3. Enter formula in top left cell of table.

    NOTE: Make sure formula refers to both input cells.

4. In first column of the table beginning in the second row, enter input values you want 1-2-3 to use for input cell 1.

5. In second column of table (to the right of the formula), enter input values you want 1-2-3 to use for input cell 2.

Create 3-Variable Table

A 3-variable table is similar to a 2-variable version, but the table range is 3D. Put formula and the three input cells outside the table. Then, the first cell in each worksheet is one of the values for the third variable. However, the formula and input cells appear in only the first worksheet.

1. Insert same number of worksheets as number of values for input cell 3.

2. Decide where to put the 3D table range. It must be in exactly the same location, in contiguous worksheets. Be sure you have enough room for the formula, input values and results.

(continued...)

CREATE 3-VARIABLE TABLE (continued)

> *NOTE: The table range will span two or more worksheets, depending on the input values for the third variable.*

3. Position the two input cells outside table. Enter a sample variable in each input cell, if desired.

4. Enter formula outside table range.

   > *NOTE: Make sure formula refers to the three input cells.*

5. Enter values for input cell 1 in first column of the table range in the first worksheet.

6. Copy these values to all worksheets in table range.

7. Enter values for input cell 2 in first row of table range in first worksheet.

8. Copy these values to all worksheets in table range.

9. Enter one input value for input cell 3 in top left cell of each worksheet in table range.

Calculate 1-Variable Table

1. Highlight (select) table.

   > *NOTE: Do not include input cell.*

2. Click **R**ange .... Alt + R

3. Click **A**nalyze .... A

(continued...)

CALCULATE 1-VARIABLE TABLE (continued)

4. Click **W**hat-if Table... **W**

5. Position cursor................................ **↑** **↓** **→** **←**
   in **N**umber of variables
   drop-down box.

6. Choose **1** .... **↑** **↓** , **⏎**

7. Position cursor in **Input cell 1** box.......... **Alt** + **1**

8. Type location of input cell 1 ....*input cell 1 location*

9. Click **OK**.. **⏎**

Calculate 2-Variable Table

1. Highlight (select) table.

   NOTE: Do not include input cells.

2. Click **R**ange ....**Alt** + **R**

3. Click **A**nalyze.. **A**

4. Click **W**hat-if Table...................................... **W**

5. Position cursor .... **↑** **↓** **→** **←**
   in **N**umber of variables
   drop-down box.

6. Choose **2** .... **↑** **↓** , **⏎**

7. Position cursor in **Input cell 1** box.......... **Alt** + **1**

8. Type location of input cell 1 ....*input cell 1 location*

(continued...)

CALCULATE 2-VARIABLE TABLE (continued)

9. Position cursor in **Input cell 2** box .... `Alt` + `2`

10. Type location of input cell 2 .... *input cell 2 location*

11. Click **OK** .... `↵`

Calculate 3-Variable Table

1. Highlight (select) 3D table range.

    NOTE: Do not include input cell.

2. Click **R**ange .... `Alt` + `R`

3. Click **A**nalyze .... `A`

4. Click **W**hat-if Table .... `W`

5. Position cursor .... `↑` `↓` `→` `←`
    in **N**umber of variables
    drop-down box.

6. Choose **3** .... `↑` `↓` , `↵`

7. Position cursor in **Input cell 1** box .... `Alt` + `1`

8. Type location of input cell 1 .... *input cell 1 location*

9. Position cursor in **Input cell 2** box .... `Alt` + `2`

10. Type location of input cell 2 .... *input cell 2 location*

11. Position cursor in **Input cell 3** box .... `Alt` + `3`

12. Type location of input cell 3 .... *input cell 3 location*

(continued...)

CALCULATE 3-VARIABLE TABLE (continued)

13. Position cursor in
    Formula cell text box .... `Alt` + `F`

14. Type location of formula cell .... *cell location*

15. Click **OK** .... `↵`

WINDOWS

Split

-Classic keystrokes-

position cursor, `/`, `W`, `W`, `H` or `V`

1. Click **View** .... `Alt` + `V`

2. Click **Split** .... `S`

3. Select **Split** type:

   • **H**orizontal .... `H`

   • **V**ertical .... `V`

4. Click **OK** .... `↵`

Clear Split

-Classic keystrokes-

`/`, `W`, `W`, `C`

(continued...)

CLEAR SPLIT (continued)

1. Click **V**iew .... Alt + V

2. Click **Clear Split** .... S

Select Scrolling Option

-Classic keystrokes-

/ , W , W , S or U

1. Click **V**iew .... Alt + V

2. Click **S**plit .... S

3. Click **S**ynchronize scrolling .... S
    (so X is displayed in box)
    to scroll views together.

    OR

    Click **S**ynchronize scrolling .... S
    (so X is not displayed in box)
    to scroll views separately.

4. Click **OK** .... ↵

    *NOTE: Press F6 to move from one window to
    another.*

WORKSHEET

Perspective

-Classic keystrokes-

`/`, `W`, `W`, `P`

1. Click **V**iew .... `Alt` + `V`
2. Click **S**plit .... `S`
3. Click **P**erspective .... `Alt` + `P`
4. Click **OK** .... `↵`

Clear Perspective

-Classic keystrokes-

`/`, `W`, `W`, `C`

1. Click **V**iew .... `Alt` + `V`
2. Click **Clear S**plit .... `S`

Freeze Titles

-Classic keystrokes-

`/`, `W`, `T`, `B` or `H` or `V`

(continued...)

FREEZE TITLES (continued)

1. Position cell pointer in one of the following locations:

    - One cell below rows to be frozen.

    - One cell to right of columns to be frozen.

    - In cell below all rows and to right of all columns.

2. Click **View** .... `Alt` + `V`

3. Click **Freeze Titles** .... `T`

4. Click **OK** .... `↵`

Clear Frozen Titles

-Classic keystrokes-

1. Click **View** .... `Alt` + `V`

2. Click **Clear Titles** .... `T`

ZOOM

Zoom In/Out

Increases/decreases display size of cells. Each time you Zoom In/Out, the display changes by 10%. The maximum size of cells is 400% and the minimum size is 25% of the normal size.

1. Click **View** .... `Alt` + `V`

(continued...)

ZOOM IN/OUT (continued)

2. Click **Z**oom In .... `Z`

   OR

   Click **Zoom O**ut .... `O`

   > *NOTE:* *To return to default setting, see **Custom Zoom**, below.*

Custom Zoom

Resets display size of cells to default setting.

1. Click **V**iew.. `Alt` + `V`

2. Click **C**ustom .... `C`

   > *NOTE:* *To change default setting, see **Change Custom Zoom**, below.*

Change Custom Zoom

1. Click **View**.. `Alt` + `V`

2. Click **Set View P**references............................. `P`

3. Click **Custom z**oom %................................... `Z`

4. Type desired number ....*number*

   OR

   Click up or down arrow...................... `↑` `↓`

5. Click **OK**... `↵`

FUNCTION DESCRIPTIONS

Lotus 1-2-3 Release 4 for Windows supports 120 new
@functions, divided into 10 different categories.
Examples are listed below.

Calendar Functions

@DATEINFO   Returns information about date.

@DAYS   Calculates number of days between two date numbers.

@WEEKDAY   Calculates day of week in date number.

Database Functions

@DPURECOUNT   Counts non-blank cells in range(s).

Engineering Functions

@BETA   Calculates Beta function for two values.

@SERIESSUM   Calculates sum of a power series.

@SQRTPI   Calculates positive square root of a value times 1.

Financial Functions

@ACCRUED   Calculates accrued interest for period interest payments.

@PAYMT   Calculates periodic payment needed to pay off loan.

@YIELD   Calculates yield to maturity.

(continued...)

170

Information Functions

@RANGENAME   Returns name of range.

@REFCONVERT   Converts column or worksheet letters (A-IV) to numbers (1-256).

Logical Functions

@ISAAF   Tests for defined add-in @function.

@ISFILE   Tests for file on disk.

Lookup Functions

@MATCH   Locates relative position of cell with specified contents.

@XINDEX   Locates contents of cell by column, row and worksheet.

Mathematical Functions

@EVEN   Rounds a value, away from 0, to the nearest even integer.

@ODD   Rounds a value, away from 0, to the nearest odd integer.

NOTE: While @Product is a mathematical function, it is listed as a statistical one. See below.

@SIGN   Determines if value is positive, negative or zero.

(continued...)

FUNCTION DESCRIPTIONS (continued)

Statistical Functions

@MEDIAN	Calculates median of values in a list.
@PRODUCT	Multiplies values in a list.
@PUREAVG	Averages values in a list (ignores text and labels).
@PUREMAX	Locates largest value in a list (ignores text and labels).
@PUREMIN	Locates smallest value in a list (ignores text and labels).

Version Manager: Information Functions

@VERSIONCURRENT	Returns name of current version for specified range.
@VERSIONDATA	Returns value or contents of specified cell in version.
@VERSIONINFO	Displays information about attributes of version.

NOTE: These functions appear under the ALL @functions category.

FUNCTION KEYS

Key	Key Name	Function Performed
F1	HELP	Accesses Help menu.
F2	EDIT	Puts Lotus 1-2-3 Release 4 for Windows in EDIT mode to enable cell contents to be edited.
F3	NAME	Displays list of names related to command or formula.
F4	ABS(olute)	In READY mode, anchors cell pointer. In EDIT, POINT and VALUE modes, changes cell or range reference from relative and absolute to mixed.
F5	GOTO	Moves to cell, named range, named object, another worksheet in same file or another active file.
F6	PANE	Moves cursor between worksheet panes.
F7	QUERY	Updates data in query table. Equal to Query Refresh Now.

(continued...)

FUNCTION KEYS (continued)

Key	Key Name	Function Performed
F8	TABLE	Repeats last range analyze what-if table command.
F9	CALC	In READY mode, updates all formulas in all active files. In EDIT mode, converts formula to value.
F10	MENU	Makes the menu bar active. Same as ALT.
Alt + F1	COMPOSE	In READY, EDIT and LABEL modes, creates international characters that cannot be entered directly from keyboard.
Alt + F2	STEP	Turns STEP mode on/off to execute macros one step at a time.
Alt + F3	RUN	Displays list of macro names for selecting a macro to run.
Alt + F6	ZOOM	Enlarges the current horizontal, vertical or perspective pane to full size, or shrinks it to its original size.

(continued...)

FUNCTION KEYS (continued)

NOTE: Not equal to View Zoom In or View Zoom Out.

Alt + F7	APP1	Accesses add-in program assigned to key.
Alt + F8	APP2	Accesses add-in program assigned to key.
Alt + F9	APP3	Accesses add-in program assigned to key.
Alt + F10	Classic Add-in	Displays Classic add-in menu.

GLOSSARY

Absolute Value
A term used in the copying process to indicate reproduction of a cell without change. Sometimes referred to as "no change."

Add-Ins
Special Programs that can be used with Lotus 1-2-3 Release 4 for Windows to extend its capabilities.

Cell
A single location on a worksheet.

Cell Address
A column letter and row number, e.g., A1 or F12.

Column
The vertical portions of the worksheet, e.g., A, B, C, etc. There are 256 columns in a worksheet.

Column Width
A term used to refer to the size of a cell. A cell may be made wider or narrower from the default size of 9 characters.

Cursor
The cell pointer.

Copying
Reproducing data from one location to another.

Data Range
The range of values used to create a graph.

Default
Settings automatically used by the program that can be modified. For example, column width settings.

(continued...)

GLOSSARY (continued)

Editing
Changing the contents of a cell.

Field Names
Column headings (labels) that appear in the first row of a database which identify the content of each column.

File
A collection of saved worksheets.

File Name
The name given to a collection of shared worksheets.

Font
Characters available in a typeface in varying sizes and styles which may be used to change the appearance of the printed worksheet or graph.

Formatting
Using special function commands to display worksheet data.

Function
A built-in formula that performs calculations or special operations.

Global
A command affecting the entire worksheet.

Graphing
Preparing a visual interpretation of data in the form of a bar, line or stacked bar graph or pie chart.

Icon
Graphics representing Lotus commands.

Label
The column and row headings or titles that begin with a letter or label prefix.

(continued...)

GLOSSARY (continued)

Label Prefix
Characters that precede the label to control label alignment.

Learn
A Lotus feature used to create macros.

Local
A command that changes a specific portion of the worksheet.

Logical Function
An @function that answers a true/false question and calculates data according to the answer.

Logical Operator
Symbols such as ><, #AND# and #OR# used in logical formulas to evaluate equality and inequality.

Macro
A series of recorded keystrokes that automates a Lotus task.

PrintGraph
The Lotus program that prints graph files.

Range
A cell or a rectangular group of adjacent cells in the worksheet.

Range Address
The location of a range in a worksheet: A3..D5.

Range Name
A name given to identify a range on a worksheet.

Relative
A term used in the copy process to indicate the automatic change of the cell references in the formula to adapt to the new location.

(continued...)

GLOSSARY (continued)

Retrieve
The process of accessing a saved file.

Row
The horizontal portion of a worksheet. e.g., 1, 2, 3, etc.
There are 8,192 rows in a worksheet.

Save
Stores a copy of the worksheet on disk.

Setup String
Characters preceded by a \ that direct the printer to print a
certain way.

Scroll
A vertical or horizontal cursor movement that displays
portions of the spreadsheet existing beyond the limits of the
screen.

Sort
The process of arranging records in the database in a
particular order according to the contents of one field.

Value
A numerical or formula entry on the worksheet used in
calculations.

Window
A software command to split the spreadsheet horizontally
or vertically into separate scrollable worksheets.

Worksheet
A columnar spreadsheet containing 256 columns and 8,192
rows used to calculate or analyze data.

(continued...)

MACRO COMMANDS AND DESCRIPTIONS

Lotus 1-2-3 Release 4 for Windows supports 250 new macro commands. These commands are divided into 11 different categories. Examples of new commands in the different categories are listed below.

Charting

{CHART-ASSIGN-RANGE}	Assigns data ranges in chart.
{CHART-COLOR-RANGE}	Assigns colors to data points in chart.

Clipboard

{EDIT-CUT}	Cuts data and formatting from worksheet to Clipboard.
{EDIT-PASTE-LINK}	Creates link between 1-2-3 and file referenced on Clipboard.

Data Manipulation

{QUERY-NEW}	Creates new database query object.
{SEND-SQL}	Sends SQL syntax string to external database driver.

DDE/OLE

{EDIT-OBJECT}	Executes verb for currently selected OLE object.
{INSERT-OBJECT}	Embeds an OLE object in 1-2-3.

(continued...)

MACRO COMMANDS AND DESCRIPTIONS (continued)

{UPDATE-OBJECT}	Updates a 1-2-3 object embedded in another application.

Dynamic Data Exchange

{DDE-ADVISE}	Specifies macro that executes when data changes in server application.
{DDE-OPEN}	Begins conversation with Windows application.

External Table Control

{COMMIT}	Commits pending database transactions.
{ROLLBACK}	Stops pending database transactions.

Interactive

{CHOOSE-MANY}	Displays dialog box and waits for user to select one or more check boxes and then choose OK or Cancel.
{CHOOSE-ONE}	Displays dialog box and waits for user to select single option and then choose OK or Cancel. The macro associated with the option then runs.
{DIALOG}	Displays custom dialog box.

(continued...)

MACRO COMMANDS AND DESCRIPTIONS (continued)

Navigation

{SELECT-APPEND}	Adds item to a collection.
{SELECT-RANGE}	Selects specified range.

Screen Control

{SET "SMARTICONS",OFF}	Turns SmartIcons palette off.
{SET "STATUSBAR",ON}	Turns Statusbar on.

User Interface

{MENU-CREATE}	Replaces current menu bar with custom menu bar.
{MENU-COMMAND-ADD}	Adds command to custom menu.

Others

{AUDIT}	Audits 1-2-3 file(s).
{SCENARIO-CREATE}	Creates new scenario.
{SEND-MAIL}	Sends mail within 1-2-3 session.
{SPELLCHECK}	Starts 1-2-3 spell checker.
{VERSION-CREATE}	Creates new version.

MOUSE POINTER SHAPES

White arrow
Moves the cell pointer and selects cells and ranges; makes a window active; moves a window; scrolls a window; opens a Control menu box; chooses commands; navigates a dialog box; selects dialog box options.

White four-headed arrow
Resizes a window with the keyboard.

White two-headed arrow
Resizes a window.

I-beam
Enters and edits data.

Black two-headed vertical arrow
Resizes a row; creates or resizes a horizontal pane.

Arrow and cell
Selects a range.

Open hand
Ready to drag or copy current selection.

Closed hand
Drag current selection.

Closed hand with cross
Drag copy of current selection.

(continued...)

MOUSE POINTER SHAPES (continued)

 Thin black cross with chart
Positions new chart.

 Thin black cross
Moves a drawn object.

 Hourglass
Wait until Lotus 1-2-3 Release 4 for
Windows finishes performing a task.

 Pencil
Creates a freehand drawing.

 Hand
Moves an object in a graph.

 Pointing hand
Displays a definition or goes to a
cross-reference in Help. Also clicks
macro buttons.

 Pointing finger
Chooses one or more drawn objects.

SMARTICONS (DEFAULT)

	Opens existing file.	[p. 97]
	Saves current file.	[p. 122]
	Prints current selection.	[p. 100]
	Displays a preview of print selection.	[p. 107]
	Cancels previous command or action when undo is set to "on."	[p. 146]
	Deletes specified data from the screen and places it on the Clipboard.	[p. 38]
	Makes a copy of specified data from the screen and places it on the Clipboard.	[p. 36]
	Pastes data from the Clipboard onto the worksheet.	[p. 100]
	Adds a set of values above, right to left.	[p. 158]
	Adds or removes bold.	[p. 10]
	Adds or removes italics.	[p. 10]

(continued...)

SMARTICONS (continued)

U	Adds or removes single underline.	[p. 10]
	Aligns data to the left.	[p. 80]
	Aligns data to the center.	[p. 80]
	Aligns data to the right.	[p. 80]
	Complete sequence in selected range.	[p. 158]
	Select several objects.	[p. 75]
	Draw forward pointing arrow.	[p. 46]
	Draw square or rectangle.	[p. 47]
	Draw circle or ellipse.	[p. 47]
abc	Draw text block.	[p. 49]
OK	Draw macro button.	[p. 80]
	Draw chart using range.	[p. 18]
	Choose next set of SmartIcons.	[p. 130]

SUMMARY OF COMMANDS

File Commands

New	Creates a new worksheet file.
Open	Opens an existing file and incorporates one existing file into another.
Close	Closes current file if Worksheet window is active. If Transcript window is active, closes it. Prompts to save modified files.
Save	Saves current file. *NOTE: If edited data was embedded in another application file, this option changes to Update.*
Save As	Saves current file using specified drive, directory, name and file type. Also used to assign password. *NOTE: If current window contains embedded worksheet, this option changes to Save Copy As.*
Protect	Assigns all worksheets in current file a password. Also changes, gets or releases network reservation for file.
Send Mail	Sends 1-2-3 data as mail using cc:Mail, Lotus Notes, Microsoft Mail (running under Windows for Workgroups, Release 3.1) or a VIM mail application.

(continued...)

SUMMARY OF COMMANDS (continued)

Print Preview Displays current selection, formatted for printing. Also used to change page layout and print selection.

Page Setup Sets headers and footers, margins, page orientation and print titles settings. Also hides and shows worksheet elements in print, saves page settings and sizes data to printed page.

Print Prints or previews selection. Also used to change page layout and number of copies to print.

Printer Setup Displays printer settings.

Exit Ends sessions and prompts to save modified files. *NOTE: If edited data was embedded in another application file, this option changes to Exit & Return, which saves changes to embedded data and returns to other application.*

File Name(s) Lists last five files viewed. Click a file name to open, without using File Open command.

Edit Commands

Undo Reverses most recent action.

(continued...)

SUMMARY OF COMMANDS (continued)

Cut

Deletes cell contents and styling, drawn objects, query tables and recorded items from worksheet and places them in the Clipboard.

Copy

Duplicates cell contents and styling, drawn objects, query tables and recorded items to Clipboard.

Paste

Copies Clipboard contents to current cursor location in Wordsheet window or Transcript window.

Clear

Deletes cell contents and styling, drawn objects, query tables and recorded items, without using the Clipboard.

Paste Special

Pastes cell contents (or styles) or query table as new query table (or worksheet data). Also used to convert formulas to values and create DDE or OLE link in the current file from another application.

Paste Link

Creates link between cells (in a file or across a file). Also used to create link between 1-2-3 and other applications.

Arrange

Positions and groups drawn objects.

(continued...)

SUMMARY OF COMMANDS (continued)

Copy Down	Copies top row of a range to other rows in the range.
Copy Right	Copies left column of a range to other columns in the range.
Copy Up (w)	Copies bottom row of a range to other rows in the range. (To display, press Shift and choose Edit).
Copy Left (r)	Copies right column of a range to other columns in the range. (To display, press Shift and choose Edit).
Copy Back	Copies from first worksheet of 3D range back through the rest of the range. (To display, press Ctrl and choose Edit).
Copy Forward	Copies from last worksheet of 3D range forward through the rest of the range. (To display, press Ctrl and choose Edit).
Insert	Inserts columns, range, rows or worksheets in current file.
Delete	Deletes columns, range, rows or worksheets in current file.
Find & Replace	Finds and replaces information in a file, query table or range.

(continued...)

SUMMARY OF COMMANDS (continued)

Go To

Locates and selects chart, drawn object, query table or range.

Insert Object

Starts another application (from 1-2-3), create data and embed data in the current 1-2-3 file.

Links

Creates DDE and OLE links between current file and other application files. Also updates file links.

View Commands

Zoom In

Increases display size of cells by 10%.

Zoom Out

Decreases display size of cells by 10%.

Custom - 87%

Resets display size of cells to default.

Freeze Titles

Freezes columns and rows, so they remain in view during scrolling. *NOTE: When columns or rows are frozen, this option changes to Clear Titles.*

Split

Divides a Worksheet window horizontally or vertically. Also displays three contiguous worksheets in perspective view. *NOTE: If the window is split, this option changes to Clear Split.*

(continued...)

SUMMARY OF COMMANDS (continued)

Set View Preferences

Hides/shows charts, drawn objects and pictures, frames, grid lines, page breaks, scroll bars and tabs. Also hides/shows edit line, SmartIcons and status bar. In addition, sets displays cell size, frame type and grid line color.

Style Commands

Number Format

Changes display of values in cells, chart axes and query tables.

Font & Attributes

Changes attributes, color of text, point size and typeface. Also styles cells, chart elements, macro buttons, query tables and text blocks.

Lines & Color

Sets line or edge style, color and pattern, border and designer frames and symbols used in line chart. Use with charts, drawn objects, query tables and ranges.

Alignment

Aligns text (in text blocks) and aligns labels and values in cells. Also changes orientation of cell contents, rotates cell contents to a different angle and wraps text in cell.

Gallery

Formats a range with a style template.

(continued...)

SUMMARY OF COMMANDS (continued)

Named Style
Saves cell styling as a named style. The named style can then be applied to other ranges.

Column Width
Determines column size in worksheet (or field size in query-table). Options include selecting number of characters, having each column (or field) automatically accommodate the widest entry and resetting columns (or fields) to the default width.

Row Height
Determines row size in worksheet (or query table). Options include selecting number of points or having each row automatically accommodate the largest font.

Protection
Turns off cell protection for a range, before the file is sealed with File Protect. Reprotects the range after it is unsealed.

Hide
Hides/shows selected columns or worksheets.

Page Break
Inserts/deletes page breaks.

Worksheet Defaults
Sets defaults for the current worksheet (including alignment, column width, font and number format). Also turns Group mode on/off, sets display of negative values and sets text and background colors.

(continued...)

SUMMARY OF COMMANDS (continued)

Tools Commands

Chart
Creates chart using the selected collection or range.

Draw
Displays a sub-menu. Sub-menu creates arcs, arrows, ellipses, lines, macro buttons, polygons, polylines, rectangles and text blocks. Freehand drawing is also allowed.

Database
Displays a sub-menu. Sub-menu appends, finds and deletes records. Also creates query database tables and cross-tabulate data. In addition, connects to, creates and sends commands to external databases.

Spell Check
Locates and adjusts duplicate or misspelled words.

Audit
Locates circular references and cells containing DDE or file links. Also finds cells containing formulas, data used in formula and formulas that use data in a specific cell or range.

(continued...)

SUMMARY OF COMMANDS (continued)

Smart_Icons Chooses icons to be displayed. Also chooses position of icons. In addition, adjusts icon size, creates custom set of icons, customizes individual icons and selects a different set of icons.

_User Setup Determines settings for several features, including autoexecute macros, automatic number formatting, default directory, drag-and-drop, error beeps, file saving, number of file names displayed on File menu, international settings, recalculation, Undo and user name.

_Macro Displays a sub-menu. Sub-menu assigns a macro to a button, controls macro recording and shows/hides Transcript window. Also opens the Macro Trace window, runs a macro and turns on Step mode.

Add-_in (Un)loads optional add-in programs.

_Range Commands

NOTE: *Range commands are available while working with data on a worksheet.*

(continued...)

SUMMARY OF COMMANDS (continued)

Version

Enters, groups, manages and views different versions of data. Also shares files and consolidates data from other users.

Fill

Enters sequence of dates, times or values in a range.

Fill by Example

Enters sequences of data in a specified range, based on pattern in the range. Also creates custom sequences.

Sort

Sorts the data in a specified range.

Parse

Separates column of labels into columns of dates, labels, times or values.

Transpose

Copies and rearranges data in a specified range. Transposes columns and rows, columns and worksheets and rows and worksheets.

Name

Creates and deletes names of ranges.

Analyze

Displays a sub-menu which creates frequency distributions, inverts and multiplies data matrices, performs what-if and regression analyses and solves problems with BackSolver and Solver.

(continued...)

SUMMARY OF COMMANDS (continued)

Chart Commands

> *NOTE: Chart commands are available while working with a chart.*

Type	Determines chart type. Also changes chart orientation, creates table of values plotted in chart and repositions plot frame.
Ranges	Assigns and plots ranges by column, row or selected range. Also plots range as an area, bar or line, and plots data against a second y-axis.
Headings	Adds, changes or positions note, subtitle and title.
Legend	Adds, changes or positions legends.
Data Labels	Creates and positions labels for data points. Also explodes slices in a pie chart.
Grids	Hides/shows x-, y- and second y-axis grid lines.
Axis	Displays a sub-menu which customizes axes, including axis type, scale, titles and units. Also positions tick marks and labels.
Name	Names (or renames) chart.

(continued...)

SUMMARY OF COMMANDS (continued)

Set Preferred — Changes default style settings to type and settings of selected chart.

Use Preferred — Changes selected chart to default style settings.

Numeric Color — Sets color and pattern for data using information entered in worksheet.

Query Commands

NOTE: *Query commands are available while working with a query table.*

Set Criteria — Defines query criteria, limits number of records displayed in query table and refreshes records in query table.

Choose Fields — Selects and arranges field in query table. Also creates a computed field.

Sort — Sorts data in query table.

Aggregate — Aggregates values in query table. Also names field containing aggregate value.

Show Field As — Renames a field in query table.

Name — Renames query table.

(continued...)

SUMMARY OF COMMANDS (continued)

Set Options

Displays sample values in Set Criteria dialog box, excludes duplicate records in query table, refreshes query table automatically and replaces original records.

Show SQL

Displays equivalent SQL command to select records in current query table.

Set Database Table

Queries a different database table.

Join

Joins additional database tables with currently selected database table or removes joined database table.

Update Database Table

Replaces records in database with edited records from query table.

Refresh Now

Updates data in query table.

Transcript Commands

NOTE: Transcript commands are available when Transcript window is active.

Playback

Runs item in Transcript window as macro.

Minimize on Run

Reduces Transcript window to icon when recorded item runs as macro.

(continued...)

SUMMARY OF COMMANDS (continued)

Window Commands

Title	Sizes and positions windows side-by-side.
Cascade	Sizes and positions windows diagonally.
Window Name(s)	Lists as many as nine open windows. A check mark indicates the active window. To make a different window active, click on the desired window name.
More Windows	Appears if more than nine windows are open. To see list of additional windows, click More Windows.

Help Commands

Contents	Displays topic categories.
Search	Lists topics matching typed word.
Using Help	Describes how to use Help feature.
Keyboard	Describes keyboard shortcuts. Also describes editing, function and navigation keys.
How Do I?	Explains how to perform common procedures.
For Upgraders	Explains 1-2-3 Classic, new features and parts of the window.

(continued...)

SUMMARY OF COMMANDS (continued)

Tutorial   Starts tutorial.

About 1-2-3   Displays release number and copyright information.

@Function Commands

List All   Lists all @functions by category. Also adds or removes @functions from menu.

SUM   Inserts @SUM into formula.

AVG   Inserts @AVG into formula.

ROUND   Inserts @ROUND into formula.

IF   Inserts @IF into formula.

TODAY   Inserts @TODAY into formula.

NPV   Inserts @NPV into formula.

INDEX

(continued...)

(continued...)

INDEX (continued)

E

F

G

(continued...)

204

INDEX (continued)

(continued...)

INDEX (continued)

N

O

P

(continued...)

INDEX (continued)

(continued...)

INDEX (continued)

(continued...)

208

INDEX (continued)

More Quick Reference Guides

At your local bookstore, or by mail.

------- ORDER FORM -------------

DDC *Publishing*

( ) Check for dealership information

14 E. 38 St., NY, NY 10016

Accept my order for the following titles at $8.95 each.

QTY.	CAT. NO.	DESCRIPTION

☐ Check enclosed. Add $2 for post. & handling & 50¢ post. for ea. add. guide.
NY State res. add local sales tax.
☐ Visa ☐ Mastercard

100% Refund guarantee

Allow 3 weeks for delivery.

No._____ Exp. _____

Name_____

Firm_____

Address_____

City, State, Zip_____